Table of Contents

Preface

Mexicans go to the United States looking for a piece of the American Dream. Americans live and retire in Mexico looking for a piece of the Mexican Dream. Go figure.

There are an estimated 2,000,000 American retirees living in Mexico, myself included. There must be a reason. Or reasons. The most publicized reason is the standard of living is lower and the dollar and euro go further for both travelers and retirees.

On a limited budget with a fixed pension or Social Security many retirees have found they can retire to Mexico and not have to work, whereas if they live in the US they not only have to scrimp on expenses but have to get at least a part time job to make ends meet.

But there are many other reasons for retiring in Mexico as well; proximity to the United States, few travel restrictions, great resorts, varied geography, friendly people and really great Mexican food to name a few.

And of course there are the well-publicized negatives which also need to be considered.

I decided when I was a teenager that I would retire in Mexico. I have always loved the people, climate and food. But that is me; you are different. Your reasons for retiring or traveling in Mexico may be entirely different than mine. Viva la diferencia!

So I can't tell you what to do; only offer some suggestions about what worked for me and what didn't. You can take advantage of my experience, as well as the experience of others, and become part of the 2,000,000. Or not.

What follows is a rather short summary of things you might find helpful should you decide to retire in Mexico. Admittedly it is not the definitive word. Some of these 100 entries may be very important for you and others much less so. As with life in general, it is always good to take the best and leave the rest. Such is life, no?

So just because I have lived, worked, and traveled in almost the entire country and now have retired here, don't just take my word for it. Get other opinions, research the information you need to know, ask those that have been here. Be open to the good, bad, beautiful and sometimes not so pretty. Look for reality, not hearsay or fantasy.

You may disagree with some of the things I say but I'm not sugar coating these 100 tips to win a popularity contest. My effort here is to tell it as I have seen it and lived it.

Besides, this is not about me; it's all about you. How to make a good informed decision is your task at hand. In fact, perhaps it is wiser to convince yourself why you should not go to Mexico.

First you should decide if retiring to Mexico is feasible for you; if not, don't bother. If, it is feasible, do your homework and research and then finally go and check it out for yourself. You can "customize and configure" your retirement and travel interests and then refine them later as you go, always leaving open the door to changes or a new and exciting adventure along the way.

And who knows? Maybe we'll meet on the beach at Tulum, the market in Uruapan or the ruins at Kohunlich. You never know, right?

Just remember there really must be something to it. All 2,000,000 of us can't be wrong…

JD Deal

Playa del Carmen, Quintana Roo, México

1) Why Mexico?

Accessibility and affordability are the most obvious reasons to consider traveling, retiring and living in Mexico.

If you are American, Mexico is one of your two neighbors. In fact, if you live in Texas, New Mexico, Arizona or California, Mexico is just across the Rio Grande or Rio Bravo as it is known here in Mexico. To get to Mexico, you can walk across the bridge, take a bus or taxi, drive a car or take a plane flight.

If you are American or Canadian and are considering retiring and/or living in Mexico, you don't have to fly around the world to get here. Conversely, when you are ready to return home, it's not that far.

Importantly the standard of living is much lower in Mexico than in the USA; roughly a half to one third depending on where you are in Mexico. This means that if you are on a fixed income, such as a pension or social security, you can live for much less than you can in the United States or Canada. For instance, to live in Austin or Houston, it might cost us as a couple $1500-2500 a month to live there. In Jalapa or Merida, that figure may be $500-1000 a month.

Additionally, Mexico has many of the same goods and services as in the United States, especially in the urban areas. These services include health and dental care, banking and ATM services, car maintenance and repair, computer and cell phone service, Wal-Mart, Burger King, etc.

Mexico offers a wide spectrum of choices and lifestyles from world class condos in Cancun to Maya huts in Chiapas. Your Mexican experience can be customized to meet your needs as well as lifestyle requirements. If you are on a fixed income and budget, you can configure your requirements to meet your budget. It's not rocket science.

For those considering retirement, the reasons above may be the difference in retiring or having to continue working or working part time in the USA. Sadly, many Americans are forced to face the fact they may have to work until the day they die. This is why the number of retirees living in Mexico has doubled in the last 10 years to over 2,000,000.

Another plus is that the Mexican government and people make it very easy for Americans and other 'foreigners' to travel in Mexico; tourism has become Mexico's largest industry. Retirees alone account for almost as much cash inflow as oil.

A Mexican tourist permit costs $25 for six months and a vehicle permit $50 for six months. All that is required is a valid passport, a valid driver's license and a current vehicle registration. And if you don't want to drive, you can fly in and take the local public transportation, which is much better and cheaper than public transportation in the United States.

OK, but what about the negatives? Certainly retiring and living in Mexico is not for everybody. For instance, if you don't like Mexicans, feel all the world should speak English and are squeamish about seeing poor people in a developing country, then Mexico is not for you. Or if you believe the mass media that all Mexicans are violent and are members of drug cartels, then you probably should stay home and continue to watch the depressing evening news.

If you cringe at the sight of soldiers with machine guns, checkpoints or mandated curfews, then don't go to Mexico or at least to those areas where problems are prevalent.

But unless you have one of the reasons above to stay away, Mexico may be for you. If you are open to new ways, a new culture and learning some Spanish, Mexico can provide a great place to live part or all of the year.

If your life could use a bit of adventure and you really don't want to work for ever, homestead or live in Africa or China, then take a little time and consider the possibility of creating your very own Mexican Dream. You won't know unless you consider the possibilities.

If I can do it, then so can you.

2) To Go or Not to Go…

The way we make decisions not only determines what we are but also who we are. Every day the quality of the decisions we make sets the course for our future and our destiny as well as our happiness. Such is the cumulative effect of our decision making and the nature of life.

There are big decisions and there are little decisions. A little decision might be what we will eat for breakfast; a big decision may be where and how we live or retire.

The most common methods of making decisions are the intuitive approach and the analytical approach. Use both strategies to make good, informed decisions.

The first consideration is feasibility; is there a "brick wall" that would prevent you from retiring in Mexico? This would be something or someone that would make it impractical for such a move. An example may be you need medical treatment in the United States that you cannot get in Mexico. Another example might be a spouse that would simply refuse to go. If you have no real brick walls, then you can proceed with your decision making process.

The intuitive or 'gut' approach relies heavily on how we feel and what we intuitively think is right or best. For instance, you may not know exactly why, but you have a 'gut feeling' that retiring in Mexico might be a good idea.

The analytical approach weighs the pros and the cons, the plusses and the minuses, the benefits and the costs; the positives and the negatives.

If the pros, plusses and benefits outweigh the cons, minuses and costs then the decision is more clearly a yes or an affirmative. If the cons, minuses and costs outweigh the pros, plusses and benefits then the answer is a no. If the results are a tie we either have a 'non-decision', a postponement of a decision or a need to gather more data and information to see if the correct decision somehow tips to one side or the other.

A common though somewhat simplistic method of making an analytical decision is the Ben Franklin T. You draw a big T on a blank sheet of paper; on the top left you write "Positive" and on the top right you write "Negative".

As you analyze your available information you write the results under the appropriate column, the plusses on the left side and the negatives on the right side. After you have gone through your information and data, you will have two filled in columns.

For example, if your decision T is "Retiring in Mexico", you might have under positives 'don't have to work', 'more free time' and 'more time to fish.' Under the negative side you might have 'won't see grandkids as often', 'will miss Bingo on Tuesday nights' and 'will miss the local football games this fall.'

As you can already see, two weaknesses of the T decision making method are the positives and negatives do not carry relative scales of importance or priority and sometimes there is no clear results pattern.

But the Franklin T method does help us sort out and track the data and helps give some idea of the direction we are headed or what information we lack.

But whatever method you choose your goal should be to make a good, well-informed decision. Go through the following chapters and keep notes, some chapters will be more relevant to your personal circumstances than others.

Also add to your Decision T as you go through the chapters

One final point. No one can make the decision analysis for you because only you know how you feel, how you think, what you want, what you need, what are your resources, what are your goals, what are your relationships with others, etc.

Your decision to retire and live in Mexico is a big one. Make it a good one!

Bon voyage! Buen viaje!

3) Sample Before You Decide

Let's assume you have just gone through your analysis or done "due diligence." There are several possibilities.

One is that your result is a clear yes. The other is that your result is a clear no. Either a clear yes or a clear no will give you an indication of what is in your best interest and how you should decide.

But quite possibly you have found a mixed result with no clear indication of what is the best course of action. You have found numerous advantages and disadvantages and it is difficult for you to come to a definitive decision. And in your "gut" you are also unsure what is best to do; part of you says yes and another part says no.

Consider this. When you go to the supermarket at times there will be a small stand with "free samples" of a new or improved product. You are given a sample in the expectation there is a certain likelihood you will buy the product and also a probability you will continue to buy the product.

When you buy a car, the salesman may say "take it home for a few days and try it out, see how you like it…" The expectation again is that you will like what you experience better than your old car and make a purchase.

If you are unsure in your decision on whether to retire in Mexico, you can continue to gather more information in hopes that additional information will tip the decision scale in one direction or the other. The best way to do this is take a trip. Go, sample and see for yourself.

It will take some of your resources, both time and money. Depending on your circumstances, you can stay for a week or up to six months. This will give you time to develop both a better intuitive feel as well as gather more data and information to help your analysis.

If you have access to an airport, you can fly. If you live near the border, you can drive or take the bus. Ideally, you can simulate an actual trip you would take if you were to retire in Mexico. Just like the sample in the supermarket or buying a new car, you can try before you buy.

Of course the more time you spend, the more information you will gather and the greater the number of your questions that will be answered. Take pictures, videos, gather printed material and bring back whatever else you find that will help you in your decision making process.

Then when you get back home you can sort through your materials, add to your analysis and take a "gut check" to see how you feel once you have sampled the real thing.

Always remember that if you decide to go and don't like it later, you can change your mind and return back home. But at least you will know.

There are no certainties in life. All of us play the probabilities and hope for the best. Making a good decision puts those probabilities in your favor.

4)The Big Picture and Scenario Planning

Perspective is everything. The broader the viewpoint, the better the understanding. The better the understanding, the better the insight. The better the insight, the better the decision, outcome and desired result.

As you consider retiring and living in Mexico, it is important to have a good understanding of "the Big Picture" or what are the most important factors or dynamics in your informed decision.

For instance, how much income you have in your monthly budget is more important than where to buy the best quality tortillas. That's not to say tortillas are not important but in your decision making process how much income you have available has a greater impact on a positive outcome than where to buy tortillas.

Priorities and the basic dynamics set the stage for your Big Picture viewpoint which will ultimately factor heavily in your final decision. I can give you my perspective and Big Picture viewpoint and you will hopefully learn new things, gain greater understanding and subsequently improved insight allowing you to make a better informed decision.

But once again, you are not me. I may love mangoes and zapotes and you may think they taste weird and prefer oranges and bananas. I may not like the beach for more than a day or two and you may love the beach and want to live there. I may love the virgin jungle and you may think there are just too many bugs and snakes for any sane human to live there.

So it doesn't matter what I think; it's what you think that counts.

Once you have a grasp of your very own Big Picture, you can do some preliminary Scenario Planning. This is simply another way of looking at the best that can happen and the worst that can happen; the best case scenario and the worst case scenario.

For instance. You may look at your limited budget and desire to live at a resort beach, such as Cancun or Puerto Vallarta. A worst case scenario is that it may cost more than you can afford and if you go there you will soon run out of money, which by the way is not a good idea if you live in Mexico.

A best case scenario may allow you to find a way to afford living in a resort, perhaps not on the beach but away from it, where the local resort workers live. This would allow you to live where you want to and be able to afford it, even though the circumstances may not be ideal.

With scenario planning, we use the best case and the worst cases anticipating that the actual reality will lie somewhere in between, which it almost always does. Scenarios give us a strong indication as to what is feasible and what is not feasible or what is practical and what is not.

At this point it may be a good exercise to consider "What kinds of information do I really need to make a good, informed decision?"

That is our challenge so let's go at it!

5)Research, Research, Research

As we have seen, an informed decision is almost always a better decision. The more and better quality information and data we have, the better we can evaluate the positives and the negatives, the costs and the benefits. The purpose is to give you accurate, objective information and not to simply reinforce your pre-existing opinions.

With the above in mind, it is best to look at as much information as possible from as many sources as possible. The easiest and perhaps now best way is to search the internet, which includes websites, portals, blogs, social networks and other accessible sources of information.

The best way to start is using a topical search through a search engine, such as Ask or Google. This will lead you to official government sites, which are useful for nuts and bolts questions such as what are you allowed to bring into Mexico or how much is the vehicle bond you need to post if you decide to drive. The answers to the above questions are "almost anything except guns, ammunition, and explosives" and "$200-400 in US currency only, depending on the year of your vehicle."

Internet research provides good information about specific questions as well as general information that is good to know, such as what have been the experiences of folks that have actually retired and lived in Mexico.

You should save pertinent information in a folder, bookmark the site, cut and paste the info to a directory that you create, etc. This way when you need to go back to review what you have found, you can easily access it.

One word of caution. Just as in print, do not always believe or trust what you see on the internet. You will find opposing opinions as well as outright lies, especially regarding anything of controversy and for some people Mexico is an ongoing controversy. It should be clear that information can be skewed to fit purposes which may be contrary to your own interests.

The good news is you can find almost anything you need to find on the internet; the bad news is you have to work at determining not only its relevance but its truthfulness.

Of course the internet is not the only source of information. You should talk to those that have lived or traveled in Mexico as well as ask others their opinion. Especially try to find folks that have direct experience in Mexico and gently pick their brains for what they know that is of interest to you.

Once again we return to the Big Picture and what kinds of information do you need to make an informed decision. Or if your decision is to go and see for yourself, what kinds of information will make your trip and initial assessment more relevant to your longer term plans.

Once you have identified these areas, you can do ongoing research until you are satisfied that you have enough information.

As an exercise, try doing research on retiring in Jalapa or Guanajuato, two very desirable mid-range cities that offer continuing cultural and educational events. These are two of my favorite Mexican cities and who knows, you might want to visit them to see how you like them.

As you can see, you are now in the process of building a "mosaic" of information to help you make a good decision. This mosaic is customized for you, based on your interests, budget, limits, etc. It is your very own mosaic.

Simply put, you are now digging deeper to see if the "Mexican Dream" is for you.

6)Ask, Ask Ask and Network, Network, Network

As previously noted, one of the best ways to gather information is to ask questions to those who know or who you think might know. In the process you will find that many people say they know or think they know but upon closer scrutiny they really don't know or just have an opinion.

Having an opinion is okay but for research purposes an opinion is often of little practical value. What you want are the hard and cold facts, especially as you first are gathering information to help you make a decision. As they used to say in the classic TV show Dragnet, "just the facts, ma'am".

As you begin your quest for the truth by asking, you will often get an answer such as "I don't know but I know someone that does know or might know." Ask them for an "information referral" which should include name and contact information such as phone and/or email address.

Contact this person and say you were referred by your acquaintance and were wondering if they would know about the question you have in mind and need to find answers to. If they do great, would they be willing to talk now, later or via email? Perhaps in person? And if they don't know, would they know someone that did know?

Sometimes you will eventually meet a dead end but sometimes you may hit a goldmine and not only eventually find a person that knows what you need to know but a person that is willing to introduce you to other people that know. This is known as networking and it can be a treasure trove of information.

As you go through this process, keep a notebook with your notes or put the information into your laptop or cell phone, perhaps using a database or contact manager. Don't forget to ask for names and contact information in Mexico as well. Your contact may say " and don't forget to look up Fred when you are down there…he works in the oilfields off Ciudad del Carmen and loves to have American visitors." You get the picture, no?

If you go to Mexico, don't forget to keep your contact log going as it may come in handy for future use. For example, "my friend Manuel lives in a little village near Molango and every Easter they have a local pageant and big fiesta and he would probably let you park your camper in his back yard."

And don't forget to thank those that have helped you and offer to help them in the future should they need it. What goes around comes around and you never know, right?

You may have heard of the concept of degrees of separation; a degree of separation being defined as someone that knows someone else. A few years back there was a theory that anyone could contact anyone else through seven degrees of separation. In other words, if you know the right seven people you can meet anyone on the planet.

Well, I was never sure about that one and was never able to test it out…but I was able to test out the power of knowing someone that knows someone. Let me give you my personal example.

A friend of mine told a friend of his that I was going to take a motorcycle trip to Mexico. This would be two degrees of separation. His friend said he knew a Mexican that lived in both the US and Mexico and so he gave me his address in Mexico. This is three degrees of separation.

Well, the guy in Mexico had a sister that I met when I went there. Four degrees of separation. I met the sister, we got married and lived happily ever after.

So you never know. You might not meet someone you marry but you might meet someone that becomes your friend, rents you a house or wants you to teach them English.

But you won't know unless you ask, ask, ask and network, network, network.

7)Mexican Attitudes Toward Americans (Gringos)

Mexican attitudes toward Americans are in a constant state of flux and continue to evolve and change. In general, the anti-imperialist "Yanqui go home" perception of the past has been replaced by a new multi-faceted opinion that continues to develop, as well as the causes and sources and attributions of those opinions.

The once-disparaging names Gringo and Yanqui have now been replaced, as in the case of Yanqui, and changed, as in the case of Gringo. Gringo, or "green go" from the American intervention years, has changed both in context and meaning.

When I first visited Mexico many years ago it was clear that Gringo was used despairingly, as a term of deprecation, sarcasm and even hate. Today the word is used regularly in all levels of society as a word that simply means American, with little or no negative connotations. Gringo has "morphed" from a negative meaning to a neutral meaning and in some cases now even a positive meaning.

The word Yanqui has all but disappeared from regular usage except to refer to the major league baseball team from New York.

Another term for American that is more common now is "Norte Americano" or North American. There still remains some resentment and bitterness when we Americans refer to ourselves as "Americanos" since the general feeling is that all that reside in North America should be called Americanos and not just we Americans.

Of course some of the lingering resentment of Americans has to do with the Mexican wars where Mexico lost Texas, Arizona, New Mexico and California. This despite the fact that in the late 1840's there were relatively few Mexicans living in these areas as most of the non-Indigenous people living there were native born.

In general Mexicans today perceive of their problems being more internally than externally driven.

The American resentment today is more often due to the perception that the United States mistreats illegal immigrants, mostly Mexican, and this remains a sore spot between the two countries. Mexican Presidentes freely chastise the American government for its continued "oppression" of Mexicans and as a tourist you will eventually hear this argument expressed indignantly.

How you reply to these assertions or "charges" is up to you but you can certainly be put in an awkward position if you vigorously support stronger border control and more stringent illegal immigrant restrictions. You might consider replying in such a manner as to diffuse the issue: "I can see your point" or "yes, we do seem to have many political problems in my country."

You will find that the resentment is almost always directed toward the politics and government of the United States and not at you as an individual citizen. Mexicans are well aware of the feeling of hopelessness that is generated by politics and government and are just as skeptical about the ineffectiveness of politicians and governments as the average American, if not more so.

There is one more very important additional factor to consider and that is that virtually everyone in Mexico now has a relative or friend living and working in the United States and so it is clear not all illegal immigrants are mistreated. It has been estimated that at least 10% of the Mexican population or over 12,000,000 Mexicans are now living in the US.

When these Mexicans return home to Mexico they bring with them stories and opinions of life in the US and in general a very positive attitude toward the US. This has done more than perhaps any other factor in changing the attitudes and public opinion that Mexicans have of the United States.

To paraphrase the vernacular, "it is what it is."

8) Adaptation, Assimilation and Acculturation

How you accept Mexican culture and assimilate into Mexican society is a very personal issue and depends primarily on you as an individual and your preferences. You will meet Americans that speak no Spanish and refuse to learn as well as refuse to go out and "mingle" with the general population. Or you will meet Americans like me that speak Spanish and live at times in areas where no other Americans live.

As a retiree in Mexico, you most likely will be somewhere in between these two "extremes." The choice is obviously yours but you may want to consider what is not only most effective and efficient but was is also most satisfying, enriching and fun for you.

For me, I see little merit in moving to, retiring in and living in Mexico trying to duplicate my life in the United States. In fact, I would go so far to say that if you do not want to experience Mexico in any form you are better off staying in the US or finding some other suitable alternative.

Acculturation does not mean you have to become Mexican nor give up your "native culture". There are tens of millions of people living in the United States and Mexico that speak both Spanish and English and have accepted both the American and Mexican cultures. I happen to be one of them. Our attitude is that if one language and culture is good than two languages and cultures must be twice as good.

Admittedly that argument may be a bit simplistic but hopefully you get my point. If you are going to spend the time, effort and resources to retire in Mexico why not take full advantage of the opportunities and experiences that will be available to you? To me this only makes sense but you as a prospective retiree will have to search your soul, and possibly that of your spouse, and determine just how you feel about acquiring a new language and new culture.

Because as with many things in life your attitude will determine your results. If you see learning a new language and culture as being a threat to your current language, that most likely will be your result. If you see learning a new language and culture as fun and exciting and, now that you are retired, something worthwhile and meaningful to do, then that will also be your result.

Perception and its corresponding attitudes are everything.

By speaking a little Spanish and understanding and respecting the Mexican culture you will make it easier on yourself. You will get along better, make more Mexican friends, be able to travel and carry out your activities of daily living easier, etc.

A useful approach is to find an interest and pursue it. It could be food, art, surfing, indigenous culture, history or pretty much whatever you chose. Go with your own flow. Not only will you find interest and entertainment but a general level of satisfaction as well. Do those things that you always wanted to do but didn't have the time.

Having the time to pursue your interests is part of the reason for retiring in Mexico, no? Besides, if "no man is an island" than why isolate yourself? Relax and enjoy; you earned it.

One other comment. You don't have to become fully bilingual and bicultural like I am. If you know several thousand words in Spanish and generally know and understand the basic culture and traditions of Mexico, you will be fine. You can adapt your level of adaptation and acculturation to your comfort level, or maybe push those limits just a bit.

Give yourself permission...go ahead and challenge yourself a little!

9) Where in Mexico?

Mexico is a huge country. I have been traveling in Mexico for over 40 years and still have not been everywhere.

If you are not sure where to go, you can travel about and see what interests you. Then when you find the area you like, you can think about settling down in a more "permanent" situation.

Clearly your decision will be a reflection of your preferences and circumstances.

Mexico has 32 states and over 3,000 municipalities. It has the Pacific Ocean on the west, the Gulf of Mexico on the east, and the Caribbean Sea on the south. It has two main mountain ridges running down the western and eastern sections with a high plateau in the middle. It has desert in the north and jungles in the south.

Mexico has thousands of small villages as well as what is often considered the most populous city in the world.

With such a wide variety of places to choose from, you may even find your curiosity piqued and want to visit several areas.

One way to start your search is to make a list of your "requirements" and look for areas that meet those requirements or needs. What you will end up with is a type of matrix with your requirements in one column and places that fit those requirements on another. You can use a spreadsheet, columnar paper or plain paper.

On your requirements side, list in order of importance or ranking of priorities those things that are relevant to you. For instance, if you are working on a tight budget, you might want to not consider expensive places to live, such as Cabo San Lucas, Ciudad Del Carmen or Playa del Carmen.

If you need to be within a day's drive of the US, you might consider Guaymas, Creel or Tuxpan, Veracruz.

If you can't take the heat and humidity, you might consider towns in the Eastern or Western Sierras.

If you really want to live near the beach, don't waste your time looking at areas in the central highlands.

Work smart. As you develop your own personal matrix you will start to eliminate regions and cities that would not be appropriate for you; no need wasting your time and energy on someplace that is not feasible for you.

Don't forget to check Google maps for an idea of terrain as well as main roads and airports.

The more research you do the more familiar you become with which areas may best suit your needs. Of course you will eventually have to go but knowing before you go will make your final choice an easier one.

Of course you may go and discover your Mexican Dream town is not what you thought it might be. But don't give up…keep trying. Your Mexican Dream may be just around the next side trip…

10. Geography

Few countries in the world have as varied a terrain as Mexico.

Western Mexico is bounded by the Pacific Ocean which includes the Baja Peninsula and the Sea of Cortez. Eastern Mexico is bounded by the Gulf of Mexico and Southeastern Mexico by the Caribbean Sea.

Northern Mexico is desert with vast expanses of sand, rock and mountains. The Sonora Desert in northwestern Mexico is one of the harshest places on Earth yet also one of the most beautiful with hundreds of square kilometers in protected park areas. The saguaro and other cactus succulents remind one of a desert garden.

The southern section is mostly jungle: the southwestern region and State of Chiapas being one area and the Yucatan Peninsula another. The Yucatan jungle is comprised of limestone rock, thick brush thickets with growth and an amazing array of animal, plant and insect life. Chiapas has mountains and valleys and flat areas of deep jungle growth.

Running north to south are two long, high mountain ranges: the Sierra Madre Occidental range and the Sierra Madre Oriental. The western or Oriental ranges tend to be dry and in many places semi-arid. The western range is well known for having the Copper Canyon, one of the steepest canyons in North America.

The Eastern Sierras receive plentiful rainfall as the moist Gulf of Mexico winds and clouds reach higher altitudes. This section is tropical and semi-tropical with lush vegetation and many streams and rivers carrying the rainfall water back to the Gulf.

In between the two mountain ranges is the highland plateau; a vast area that is somewhat dry but also has some of Mexico's most productive farmland. Mexico City, one of the world's largest cities, is located on this plateau.

In summary, most of Mexico is desert, jungle, coastal, mountainous or central plateau.

One of the interesting things about travel in Mexico is the great variety of geographical terrains that can be found in relatively short distances. For instance, from Mexico City to Vera Cruz City is only four hours by bus or car and yet one goes though high plateau, mountains, rolling hills, flat lower plains and eventually coastal or beach areas.

Because of the great diversity of geographic zones there appear a great variety of geographic formations. From high Sierra Mountain and volcanic peaks, large mountain caverns, waterfalls pouring through lush tropical forests, fertile rolling hill farmland, swamps and some of the most famous beaches in world on the Riviera Maya on the Caribbean coast.

In the past some of the more interesting geologic sites were found in remote areas that required four wheel drive trucks or perhaps even helicopters to gain access. However in the past 10 years Mexico has greatly expanded its highway system and now many previously inaccessible areas are accessible by car. This does not necessarily mean that there are available hotels and restaurants but often there are cabins or small, simple hotels near the more popular natural phenomena.

The retired tourist has several options. If you have the funds, you can drive and take a trip around the entire country in four or five months. By exploring you can find which areas are more to your liking as well as pocketbook. My favorite areas are the eastern Sierras near Tamazunchale, the western Sierras near Uruapan, the Copper Canyon at Batopilas and the Caribbean coast near Xcalak and Bacalar.

Once you settle into an area you can take day or overnight trips to explore the surrounding countryside. Ask the locals what they would recommend; most folk are more than happy to give you some pointers. Like the ancient Indigenous ruins, some of the best ones to visit are some of the least well known.

You may even find an area that is more appealing to you and decide to move there. One of our favorite places is Xico near Coatepec in the state of Veracruz. I would not at all be surprised if one day we set up another home base there.

Decisions, decisions, decisions…

11) Big Cities

Big Cities in México include: México City, Monterey, Guadalajara, Pachuca, Tampico, Mérida, Vera Cruz, Cancún, Oaxaca, Puebla, Tijuana, Ciudad Juárez, and Reynosa. These cities each have a population of at least one million.

My favorite Big Cities in Mexico are Vera Cruz and Merida.

Everything in the big cities is bigger and more extreme allowing for very obvious advantages and disadvantages. There is a strong growth tendency in large Mexican cities because the cities contain most of the country's jobs and economic base.

Salaries and wages tend to be much higher in the bigger cities but so too does the cost of living, depending on the area. In general it will cost more to live in a big city, especially to live well.

Larger cities have affluent areas as well as large poor, marginalized areas with substandard housing. Most of the poorer areas are found on the outskirts and may be characterized as "shanty towns" with not only economic problems but social problems as well.

Cities such as Acapulco and Cancun will have very nice residential areas but also large "colonias" or neighborhoods where the poor and working class live out of necessity. In between the affluent and the poor are areas that are not only physically in between but economically in between as well.

These areas are more affordable and offer the retiree more possibilities though few foreign retirees live in these areas.

The primary advantage of bigger cities is the obvious economic base. With this strong base come other advantages such as the availability of shopping malls with American chain stores. If you get homesick you can always go hang out at Wal-Mart, Costco or Burger King.

You will also find very well educated people in the major cities which is often not the case in smaller towns and villages. If being around "sophisticated" people is important to you, you should consider large cities.

Public transportation in major cities tends to be good but not fancy. Subways, busses, taxi vans and taxis are abundant and provide regular and inexpensive service. Regional transportation is available at centralized bus stations and some airports in larger cities offer international flights.

Major cities also offer a variety of open air markets in different areas on different days of the week. Many Mexicans prefer to shop daily in these markets buying only what they need for the day taking advantage of the fresh fruit and vegetable availability.

With the economic base comes support for the arts and cultural events. Local newspapers and websites will carry a listing of these events, many which are free or at a nominal cost.

The disadvantages of big cities are as numerous as the advantages. Crime, smog, garbage, inadequate drainage and sewers, congested traffic, crowded public transportation, and higher rents are considerations as well.

It is just as important to consider the disadvantages as well as the advantages. For example, in Mexico City there are certain days when the air pollution is very bad and the local government will recommend that citizens remain indoors. If you have a lung or breathing problem Mexico City may not be for you.

There are also differences among larger cities, some are more "livable" than others. Some have more cultural activities available and others offer more shopping alternatives. Specific research may help you understand these difference but eventually you will most likely have to go and see for yourself.

One good possible alternative is living in a small town outside of a major city. That way you can take advantage of the shopping and cultural activities on an as needed basis and avoid many of the harsh realities of big city life. I have found this to be a good compromise optimizing the advantages and minimizing the disadvantages.

One has to determine one's own formula for the quality of life. My prejudice and bias tends to be against big cities, even in the United States. I prefer to hear birds sing rather than hear the roar of traffic. I do enjoy going to art galleries and museums and the variety of foods offered in larger cities. I also enjoy a break from the jungle and back country; at times air conditioning, a shower and a clean, modern hotel room is what the doctor ordered.

You need to make your own decision. Perhaps you need the amenities offered by the bigger cities. Continue keeping your requirements in mind and match them to the advantages and disadvantages of life in the big city to help you focus on your decision.

Keep at it…you have made a great start!

12. Small Cities

Smaller cities offer a good alternative from big city and small town rural life. Small cities can offer many advantages with mitigated or lessened disadvantages. As with most extremes, the "middle way" is often the best way.

Small cities include Tuxpan, Poza Rica, Jalapa, Orizaba, Ciudad del Carmen, Champotón, Valladolid, Chetumal, Palenque, Ocosingo, Uruapan, Puerto Vallarta, Los Mochis, Tama zúnchale, Ciudad Valles, San Luis Potosí, Guanajuato, Tehuantepec, Chiapa de Corso and Oxcoxcalb.

My favorite smaller cities are Valladolid, Jalapa, Uruapan, Oxcoxcalb, and Ocosingo.

Some smaller cities such as Valladolid and Guanajuato have colonial style centers that retirees and tourists find appealing. You can go to a local coffee shop and have a "café lechero" and chat with some fellow compatriots. Some cities like Guanajuato may have universities that offer a steady stream of cultural events and festivals that are open to the general public.

A real plus of the smaller city is that houses and apartments located in the central areas are not in major crime zones and are more affordable than in the larger cities. In fact there may be numerous outlying or suburban "colonias" that also offer more affordable but adequate housing. A cheap bus ride from these areas will take you to the central area and numerous amenities.

I have lived in a number of smaller cities and personally find them more appealing than the larger cities and a good alternative to towns and villages. People tend to be friendlier in smaller cities and there is not the hard edge often found in major metropolitan centers.

In recent years many major chain stores such as Soriana, Chedraui, Costco and Wal-Mart have moved to these smaller cities. Their stores may not be mega-stores or "super centers" but they do provide almost everything you could want or need. They are always located on busy thoroughfares with easily accessed public transportation.

Another advantage is that these smaller cities have hospitals and medical and dental care available that is usually more affordable than in the larger cities; smaller towns often do not and may not have clinics as well.

As you get familiar with small city life you will also find good bakeries, restaurants and open air markets or "tianguis" that you will frequent. Folks tend to be more open and less distrustful than in the major cities and will not hesitate to give you a recommendation or directions. As usual, don't forget to express your sincere gratitude.

Once you learn the major boulevards and bus routes you can become oriented and travel throughout the smaller city with little or no problems. This is not the case in a major city such as Mexico City or Monterey where one could spend a lifetime and still not be truly familiar with the multitude of different areas.

You may also find it easier to make friends in the smaller cities and larger towns especially if you are friendly and outgoing. Obviously a few friends can make the difference in your experience and in the quality of your life.

As you can see, when it comes to cities, my preferences tend toward the smaller cities like Jalapa, Valladolid and Uruapan and away from major metropolitan areas such as Mexico City, Guadalajara and Puebla. Of course there will be those that will totally disagree so once again I can only say this is my opinion and certainly not an absolute fact. Many retirees and expatriates find life in the bigger cities both exciting and rewarding; listen to any input you can get and make your own decision.

Next we will take a look at the smaller towns and villages. Keep your requirements and preferences in mind as you expand your perspective and continue to look at the Big Picture.

13. Small Towns, Villages and Farms

To some, small towns, villages and the rural areas of Mexico offer the best quality of life to be found in Mexico. I largely agree but would also assert that for many life in these areas is simply not practical nor desirable. Small town and rural life has many advantages but it would be hard to classify it as idyllic, though some may characterize it that way.

Small towns and villages include Molango, Amatlan, Tulum, Puerto Angel, Cozumel, Roca Partida, Jilitla, Tihusuco, Chicontepec, Alvarado, Catemaco, La Venta, Escarcega, Tamiahua, San Blas, Chicontepec and Creel.

My favorite small towns are Molango, Chicontepec, Amatlan, Creel and Tamiahua.

Of course we are looking here at a vast differences among towns; some may have a population of 50,000 and others less than 500. We could endlessly slice and dice and categorize but for our purposes here you are simply trying to understand the bigger picture and should you focus your efforts on a big city, small city or town.

In many small towns in Mexico you will find no tourists, retirees or folks that speak English. On the other hand, you can live in a tourist town like Tulum and not have to speak Spanish at all. Not only will you see many Americans but also Canadians, Germans, Russians, Spaniards, French, Italians, Martians, etc.

There are of course many areas in Mexico that are totally rural and even villages are few and far between. The rural areas are like the Big Cities; "extreme" in that what they offer the tourist or retiree is extreme.

The very small towns located in rural areas are unsurpassed in beauty and in some instances are virtually unspoiled. This is not so much out of ecological concern but from the fact that natural resource exploitation is not cost effective. Whatever natural resources are available are costly to extract and may not return a profit. This has served as a positive influence as it has protected many areas that otherwise would not be protected.

Not only will you not find locals that speak English, in some areas they may not even speak Spanish or speak limited Spanish. Tourist services are non-existent and many other services such as pharmacies and medical clinics do not exist as well. Sometimes bad roads can make accessibility limited especially in bad weather.

Local food is sometimes abundant and cheap but forget about finding fine whiskeys or computer accessories at the local stores.

The cost of living is often much lower than in the larger towns or cities but also the wages are much lower as well. Most younger Mexicans that live on farms or in very rural areas leave them at some point to look for a "better" way of life in the cities or in the US. Sometimes they return with their earnings and build houses and start farms. Other times they only return for brief periods to visit their families during the holidays. Life on the farm is tough, unpredictable and provides very limited opportunity.

Of course the opportunities are limited if you are looking to work or start a business. As a retiree or "turista" you are looking to do neither and so "business opportunities" is not in your requirements matrix. Rural Mexico is poor with most of the very poorest areas.

For many like myself the rural areas offer many distinct advantages found nowhere else. The people are very friendly and though wary of strangers and outsiders, may become very good friends once you get to know them. The food is often very good with fruits, vegetables and meats not only farm fresh but at very reasonable prices. If natural beauty is important to you, you will find none better than the rural areas.

And just as the town dweller can have access to a nearby town, the rural resident can have access to the small town. This means you can go once a week into town or once a month to the nearest city and see a movie, buy your medicines and get that bottle of whiskey.

What you will find is that rural Mexicans are mostly very good, honest hardworking people. You will also find they have little or no education and are unfamiliar with many of the ways of the outside world, especially those that have remained in the areas where they were born.

Of course apartments, condos and luxury homes are non-existent though you may find rooms, small houses or palapa huts available for rent. The clear advantage of living in the country is the standard of living is the lowest in Mexico and the cheapest. And depending on the area you look at, the cost of living may be one of the lowest in the entire North American continent.

So when we look at towns and villages, we have to emphasize location, location, location as well as regional context.

Once again you can see that no place is perfect. When someone says they have found the "perfect" place it simply means that they have found a place that best suits their needs and requirements, whatever those may be.

Since we are all different, we all have a different concept of what constitutes the ideal or perfect.

They aren't for everybody, but towns, villages and farm areas may be your "perfect" place. That is, if you can do without Dominos, KFC and Dollar General.

14. Retiree Colonies

Some retirees are faced with the stark reality that they can no longer live on their retirement funds with the same standard of living as when they were working. Property taxes, medical bills, insurance and so on just keep going up. For them, the retiree developments found in Mexico offer an appealing alternative to downscaling their standard of living in the US.

Cozumel, Guadalajara, Cabo San Lucas, Escondido and other areas offer an upscale version of the Mexican dream.

In these areas the equivalent modern home will cost about half what it would in Austin or Atlanta and a quarter or even less than in San Jose or Newton. Many of these areas are gated communities with private security and all the amenities of back home but at a lesser cost. These areas are especially popular with the "Snowbirds" or those that live in cold climate areas during the summer and go south for the winter.

The advantages are clear for those that can afford it but these advantages come at a price and usually a relatively expensive one. If your strategy is to sell your home, buy another home and live off your equity and pension, this might present a good option for you. Do your research and examine the prices and you will get an idea of whether it might be appropriate for you. A condo in Playa del Carmen will be much cheaper than a condo in Sausalito.

One disadvantage may be being surrounded by other people similar or just like you. This may be appealing or perhaps not, perhaps simply living in a different country in a new place is enough adventure for you.

But for my tastes, as you can guess, these areas are not appealing because you miss out on much of the positives that Mexico has to offer; language and culture to name two big ones. You can live in an enclave such as Akumal if you like but don't expect to be invited to any fiestas by the working locals unless your gardener or cook simply wants to be polite.

I don't mean to be sarcastic but the idea of missing out on the best that Mexico has to offer does not sound appealing to me. It's like eating pancakes three times a day or swimming in a chlorinated hotel pool on a Caribbean beach. Why?

So maybe you will learn some Spanish trying to explain to your cook how you want your poached eggs or showing your gardener how you want your gardenias trimmed. But for my peso I would rather eat a delicious chile relleno in the Coatepec market anyway. To each his own? You may have your cocktail party but I would rather drink a beer and watch kids break a piñata at a local birthday party.

My guess is that many retirees join retirement communities simply because someone they know did and so other alternatives are not considered. Just because your sister and her husband moved to a condo community in Cabo San Lucas does not mean that is your only option. But by all means, go for a visit and check it out.

But before you decide to move in near them, look at the other alternatives. The Mexican Dream is vast and wide and you want to be sure the decision you make is best for you. Listen to your sister, listen to me, and listen to others that have an opinion. But again, in the end, it's your decision so make it work best for you.

By the way, have you ever heard of Bacalar and the Lake of Seven Colors? I met some Americans living there. Check it out…

15. Homebases: There's No Place Like Home

As a teenager, I would camp on the ground, sleep on kitchen floors or on picnic tables in parks. Now that I am much older, I find that much harder to do. And like many retirees in Mexico, I find the best solution is to have home bases on both sides of the border.

A home base can be defined as a place you can go and stay a while; a day, a month or three months. You do not have to own these "homes" although that is a possibility. Home bases can be with friends, relatives or places you rent. They can be large or small but they are place you can rest, clean up, leave your stuff and then move along to the next steps of your journey. I have and use a dozen of these in both the U.S. and Mexico.

One advantage of having a home base is cost; a cheap hotel room in the U.S. runs $60 dollars and even in Mexico perhaps $30 dollars. A week's travel including hotel, gas and meals can burn up your monthly pension check.

It's also convenient. Crossing the border and having a place to go and stay means you aren't constantly looking for a hotel late at night or having to make reservations with your credit card. When staying with friends or family it's always good to let them know beforehand although many will say "stop in any time." Of course if you own or rent a house or cabin or hut you can arrive any time, a true advantage.

You should not minimize the idea of having a place to store your things. We have pots, pans and dishes in a half dozen places so we don't have to pack them up and lug them around each time we go. It also means that you can transport other things rather than just the essentials; remember if you retire in Mexico you will still go back to the U.S. several times a year.

Keep a list of things you need for your return trip.

You also need to have "permanent" addresses for travel even if you are a gypsies like we are and rarely stay in the same place for more than several months even though we may return to the same place several times each year.

We have found that when staying with friends or relatives one or two weeks is sufficient. If you stay longer, you may become a burden, though good friends and family will often not tell you so. Don't forget to take small gifts, chip in on food expenses, prepare meals and do chores and bring along your many tales of your adventures on the road. Also show your latest photos and videos, momentos and encourage them to come for a visit.

Simply put, for many staying in a fancy hotel is not an adventure; sleeping on someone's couch in a different world is. Most folks seldom if ever leave home and are certainly not as fortunate as you to be able to retire, travel and explore like you can.

Many retirees will have a small house or condo in Mexico and another in the United States and simply go back and forth every 6 months. This works well for them and eventually we may do that but for now I get the traveling bug after staying more than a month in any one place. I traveled in various parts of the world as a teenager and have had the travel bug ever since; but you certainly don't have to follow my crazy ways!

So if you decide to retire in Mexico not only do you need to decide where to go in Mexico but where to return to the U.S. or wherever you are from. So don't forget those home bases...

16. Regular Travel Back and Forth

Let's take a look at an example of a Big Picture issue that needs consideration: travel to and from Mexico.

You will enter Mexico on a tourist permit that allows you to stay up to 180 days. Later on you can consider the possibilities of becoming an immigrant or even a naturalized citizen, but initially you will enter on a tourist permit. Virtually all retirees living in Mexico use this permit.

The tourist permit allows you to stay up to 180 days or almost six months and then you are required to physically leave Mexico for at least 72 hours or three days before you are allowed to return. How you leave and return will depend on where you live in Mexico, where the nearest border is, whether you will want to visit family and friends in the US, your budget, etc.

Let's take an example and imagine you have retired to Cancun, Quintana Roo, and an area very popular with both tourists and retirees.

Most likely you will arrive in Cancun by air; to drive to Cancun from Brownsville, Texas is a four day drive or from San Diego, California perhaps a five or six day drive. When you purchase your airline ticket you will need to make a reservation for your return, decide where and how long you will stay, etc.

Importantly you will need to figure the costs of your travel in your budget; flying is not cheap, hotels and meals in the United States are not cheap, and so on.

There are other considerations as well. Easter Week and Christmas are tough times to travel in Mexico; plane flights are booked, hotels are filled, the crowds make moving around more problematic and so on. So most likely you will want to travel either before or after these peak periods.

If you travel by bus you will also want to make reservations.

By car, you have more flexibility but still have to consider the specifics.

A bit of planning and foresight can save you both time, money and hassles.

By the way, it is important to know that both your entry and departures in Mexico are not only stamped in your passport but also are recorded by computer. So if you plan on living in Mexico you will want to abide by all the laws, rules and regulations so you will not have problems when you return. The requirements are minimal but there are some requirements.

Now is a good time to get out your map of Mexico or pull it up on your computer and take a look at the really big picture. Find Cancun, Tijuana and Matamoros. Also go from Cancun down the Caribbean coast to Chetumal, the capital of Quintana Roo located on the border with Belize. Chetumal is a five hour bus ride from Cancun, much shorter than a four day drive to Texas.

By expanding your perspective and seeing the Big Picture, you can see that you can leave territorial Mexico for three days or more in Belize and then return with a renewed 180 day tourist permit. By viewing the Big Picture you have expanded your options, quite possibly saving you much time and money.

Of course you do not have to stay the full six months; you are free to come and go as you please, or are able. You will find sometimes that you stay only several months and other times the fully allotted time for your tourist permit. This flexibility allows you to plan ahead according to your individual needs…it's really a pretty good system compared to travel in other countries.

And another reason you should seriously consider thinking of living and retiring in Mexico.

17. The Tourist Permit

You will enter Mexico on a tourist permit that is validated by your U.S. Passport. If you don't have your passport, get it.

Officially the tourist permit is known as "Forma Migratoria Multiple" or more simply "permiso de turista." The cost is $25 dollars for 180 days or almost 6 months. Note that the time allowed is 180 days which is not quite six months.

If the immigration official asks you how much time you need reply 180 days or six months. There is another permit for a week only but this will not apply to you.

The form is rather simple and in fact the Tourist Permit process is as simple as it gets, perhaps as simple as crossing any border in the world. The form requires your name, birthday, sex, marital status, passport number and mode of travel. That's it.

You should understand that the immigration official will check your passport on the computer, like running a credit card, to see if you have any outstanding arrests, warrants, lawsuits, prior offenses, criminal record, etc. Of course you don't so that won't be a problem.

Since the tourist permit is a privilege and not a right, you can in fact be denied entry, so it is important that you keep your record "squeaky clean". Upon leaving Mexico you will show immigration your tourist card and passport to cancel your permit. Your stamped passport will show both your entry and departure in territorial Mexico.

Make sure you cancel your permit since as a retiree you will want to reenter Mexico at a future date. You will surrender your tourist permit to the immigration officials as you leave.

You are required by law to stay out of Mexico for 72 hours or three days though you will hear of many turistas turning around and applying immediately for another permit. I have not heard of tourists or retirees being denied a permit for not staying out of Mexico for at least three days but you need to know the law.

If there is ever any question, your stamped passport will be proof that you entered and departed legally and on time.

Your tourist permit and passport will be your official forms of identification during your stay in Mexico. Additionally if you drive, you will be required to have a current valid driver's license from the U.S. As with all your important papers, guard your tourist permit in a safe place.

That's it. It's really as simple as it can get and it shows you how open and welcoming the Mexican government is to allowing you to visit as a tourist.

If you travel by plane you will be charged the tourist fee when you purchase your ticket. The stewardess will give you the form to fill out before you land. As you pass through immigration you will present the form to immigration.

If you are just crossing by land to a border city you will not need a tourist permit; but if you go anywhere in the interior you will.

You can also get a work visa if you work and a migrant visa if you establish permanent residence but these need not concern you initially. Most retirees simply use the tourist permit.

You can find out more details by doing an internet search on the Mexican government website.

One final word. Behave yourself, don't get into trouble, obey the laws and once again cancel your permit upon your departure. It's a great system so don't lose your privileges!

18. The Vehicle Permit

If you drive past the border into the interior of Mexico you will be required to get a vehicle permit. This is known officially as "Permiso de Importacion Temporal de Vehiculos". You will get this permit when you get your tourist permit.

You will be required to show a valid current vehicle registration and a valid driver's license along with your valid passport. These must be current.

You will also be required to post a refundable bond of $200-400 that will be refunded upon your departure as you leave provided you leave prior to the 180 day limit. The exact amount depends on the year of your vehicle. The limit date will be in the upper right hand corner of your permit. This bond is officially known as "Recibo de Deposito de Dinero en Garantía por la Importación Temporal de Vehículos."

Your vehicle identification number (VIN) will be registered as well as the date and model of your vehicle. This will be taken from your valid vehicle registration.

Copies of your passport and current driver's license will become a part of your vehicle permit file. You will be given an import permit paper with a windshield sticker as well as a receipt for your bond. Place the sticker in your front windshield directly in front of your rearview mirror.

This sticker will allow police and transit officials to immediately see that you have complied with the regulations for temporarily importing your vehicle. And you will be checked. Your permit will initially be verified at the immigration check usually 30 or 40 kilometers from the border crossing on the highway into the interior.

You are required to show your tourist permit and vehicle permit to police, transit police and soldiers when requested. You will also be required to show your driver's license to verify that it is current. You are not required to hand over your driver's license to officials, simply show it.

Upon departure you will need to cancel your vehicle permit at a border crossing. There is a specific drive-by booth near the immigration offices where you must do this. The official will take pictures of your license plate, vehicle identification number, remove the sticker from your windshield and issue you a cancellation receipt. You take this receipt along with your vehicle bond receipt inside to the immigration offices and they will refund your bond deposit.

You should cancel your tourist permit at the same time.

That's it. It's clear and simple.

A few additional comments.

Insurance is not required to import a vehicle into Mexico however if you have a newer model vehicle, it is your first trip or you are only going for a short time you should consider it. There are strong opinions about insurance coverage not being worthwhile as it is very hard to get a claim covered in case of an accident.

You and family members are allowed to drive your vehicle but others are not. Don't press your luck by loaning your vehicle out to others; just simply state that it is against the law for others to drive your vehicle.

Don't even think about selling or trading your vehicle although you may have a number of Mexican citizens that are interested in purchasing it. The legalization process is complicated, expensive and time consuming. If you sell your vehicle illegally you can lose your reentry status. Or worse.

Stay "squeaky clean" with all the rules and regulations regarding your vehicle as well as with your tourist permit. Remember that should you retire in Mexico you will be entering and leaving at least several times a year and you do not want to jeopardize your status.

The requirements and laws are consistent over time but if you have not taken a vehicle to Mexico before you will want to do an Internet search and read all the finer details on the official government website.

In my opinion, driving a vehicle is the best way to travel, see and experience Mexico. Just make sure you do it right…

19. Crossing the Mexican Border by Car

If you plan to enter Mexico by car, you will need to do a bit of planning beforehand.

If you are only planning to stay for the day or remain along the border, you will not need to get vehicle and tourist permits.

If you plan to drive to the interior more than twenty miles or so past the border, you will need to get both vehicle and tourist permits. You will also be inspected so you should know what you are allowed to take and what not to take.

Additionally, you will need to plan ahead as to where you will stay on your first night as it is not advisable to drive in Mexico after dark, especially along the border. The first reason is the well-publicized violence that is more prevalent in the border areas especially after dark. Dark includes early morning as well. The second reason is that many Mexican roads are not well marked and may have numerous potholes and other road hazards making nighttime driving more hazardous especially in rainy weather.

So plan ahead where you will spend the night. You can spend the night on the U.S. side of the border, cross fairly early, say nine o'clock and drive to an interior city to spend the night. Or you can cross in the afternoon, get your permits and spend the night in a border city hotel before continuing your trip the next day.

As you cross the bridge to Mexico you will pay a toll fee of about $3. As you enter the Mexican customs booths you may see a long line of tractor trailer trucks in the right lanes. Simply pass them in the left hand lane.

Your first stop will be a gate where your vehicle will be photographed and later the gate will be raised and you can proceed. You will then see a customs official direct you to the appropriate lane for your inspection.

Not all custom officials speak English but some do speak some English. They will ask you a series of questions, such as where are you going, how long will you stay, what are you taking, what is your line of work, etc. Answer truthfully; you have no reason to not tell the truth.

You may or may not be asked for your passport. If asked of course comply.

When asked what you are taking simply state used personal and domestic items for your use. The officials may ask you to open your trunk or pick-up bed cover and of course comply. These inspections are usually very quick and superficial but you may be asked to take out your suitcases and put them on the benches for inspections. You should comply with all requests.

You may on very rare occasions be asked to get out of your vehicle with your pet and allow a dog to inspect your car. The dog will be sniffing for chemicals used in the manufacture of methamphetamines, but of course you will not be carrying any so the dog will not find any.

When asked about your work say you are retired and no longer work. The purpose of your trip is pleasure and you will enter as a tourist. Retirees have a "special status" since they have savings and a source of income, will not be working, will not be involved in commerce, are not likely to do anything illegal, etc.

When asked about your destination tell them where you are going and for how long. For instance, "Acapulco for six months."

If you have pets they may ask to see your pet papers, though usually not.

After the inspection you will be asked to proceed forward where Mexican Army soldiers will ask you a few questions, again where are you going, how long you will be staying, what is your line of work, etc. They may ask to see what you are carrying but usually not. You will then be told to proceed where you will park outside the immigration offices to get your tourist and vehicle permits.

About twenty or thirty miles down the highway to the interior you will go through another immigration checkpoint. You will be asked to show your permits and also your passport. As usual, comply. You may be asked to pull over to an area for inspection which you will of course comply.

You may be asked if you paid any taxes on any of the stuff you are carrying. Simply reply "no". Mexicans that live in the United States and drive back into Mexico in vehicles registered in the U.S. may be required to pay duties or taxes on what they bring into Mexico. You may be asked this question again at roadblocks or even be stopped by transit police and asked the same question.

Some of these police and other officials may be trying to determine if you are a "real tourist" or not; a real tourist being a U.S. citizen. Some officials may ask Mexican citizens for a bribe; you may also be asked, though not often. You can explain that you are a tourist, you have already been inspected at the border, you did not pay any taxes on what you are carrying and all the items you have are for your personal use.

Frankly put, if a Mexican citizen complains about an official soliciting a bribe most likely the complaint will go directly to the official's superior, who in fact may be receiving part of the bribe. As a U.S. citizen your complaint could be taken to the U.S. Consul with the unscrupulous official losing his or her job. Justly or not, there is a difference.

I drive across the border three or four times a year and it has been many years since I have had to pay a bribe. Just be patient and take your time; eventually you will be told to proceed on your way. Expect it to happen and know in advance what you are going to say.

As you can see, the process is straightforward, quick and efficient, often taking an hour or less for inspections and permits. Know what you are allowed to carry into Mexico, know the requirements for your permits, and be cooperative and courteous.

Be patient and do everything "by the book" After several crossings it will become "second nature."

20. Driving in Mexico

Driving in Mexico is one of those topics that people have very strong opinions about; either they love it or hate it. In my opinion it is the best way to travel in Mexico although the bus system is very good and I have traveled many places by bus. But I have driven throughout Mexico and had very few problems and none of significance.

Driving in Mexico is largely a matter of common sense and taking your time.

You also have to consider where you are living in Mexico before you make your decision. If you are planning to live in Playa del Carmen or San Cristobal de las Casas it can be a very long drive to the nearest U.S. border; up to a week's drive in some instances.

As a rule of thumb, if you are afraid, anxious or very worried about driving in Mexico: don't. Go by plane and bus and get a feel for the country first and then on subsequent trips you can consider driving. You can also rent a car in major metro areas and see firsthand for yourself how it is to drive in Mexico; another example of sampling beforehand.

You will find that drivers in Mexico are not as courteous as those in California or Texas but more courteous than those in New York or Massachusetts. There are probably no drivers anywhere that are better drivers than the truck drivers of Mexico. Taxi drivers are also generally very good drivers as well.

When an oncoming car or truck flashes their lights, it means there is an accident or stalled vehicle ahead. After passing the obstacle, you can return the favor by flashing your lights to oncoming traffic.

The advantages of driving are many as well as significant: you can carry more stuff, come and go as you please, gasoline is readily available although at the time of this writing more expensive than in the U.S. Many very rural areas have little or no public transportation and having a vehicle can make a total difference in your quality of life and experiences there.

The disadvantages of driving are the roads are sometimes not very good, repairs and parts in some areas can be problematic, in certain areas driving after dark can be dangerous, in some areas the police may stop you for no reason, etc.

You will hear stories of drivers being crazy in Mexico City but you hear the same stories about drivers in Boston, New York and LA.

The first rule is avoid night time driving especially in the northern states. This is not optional. The later you drive at night, the greater the likelihood you will be assaulted by the bad guys and in some areas they make the rules and more so at night. Additionally many roads have potholes and are poorly marked making visibility a problem especially in bad weather.

In southern Mexico the nighttime rule is not as hard and fast but only for the early nighttime hours. Late night and early morning driving except in emergencies should be entirely avoided. If you have to stay late somewhere, spend the night.

To avoid problems with the transit police, local police and federal police, obey all the traffic signs and speed limits. This may be a bit difficult as you obey the speed limit and local drivers are honking their horns at you, but so be it. You do not want to give the police any legitimate reason for pulling you over. If you feel you can't deal with it, don't drive.

Use your mirrors and turn signals whenever you make a turn or change lanes.

If you plan on driving in Mexico City, there will be certain no drive days when you are not allowed to drive, depending on the last digit on your license plate. It does not matter if you are a tourist, you will be stopped. Know before you go.

Urban and heavy traffic driving can be particularly hectic but it's that way everywhere. Just be patient, drive slowly, obey the traffic signs, and ignore angry shouts and honking horns and you will be fine.

You also have the option of buying a vehicle in Mexico but you should not consider this option until you have lived in Mexico for a while. Vehicles in Mexico are generally more expensive to purchase and if you take your Mexican vehicle across the border to the U.S. you will have to get special insurance and so forth.

Make sure your vehicle is reliable and in good shape mechanically and don't forget the tires and brakes. You do not want to take a brand new or luxury vehicle to Mexico as it is a greater target for thieves. An older car or truck that is in good shape mechanically with a bit of rust and peeling paint is your best bet.

Whether to drive or not is one of the biggest decisions you will make if you retire and live in Mexico. Make sure the decision you make is the right one for you.

21. Car and Truck Repairs (and Parts)

Mexico has some truly great car mechanics also known these days as auto technicians. They are not only very good at removing and replacing worn or damaged parts but also good at diagnosing what is wrong in the first place. And if a part is not easily available, they often can fix the part or figure out a way to make it work.

Mechanics usually apprentice as young boys cleaning up, taking parts off junk cars and doing some of the more routine "busting nuts" jobs. As they learn more, they begin to do brakes, tune ups, services, fluid changes, etc. As new makes and models come out they learn by doing and rarely use manuals or electrical diagrams.

Every town of any size will have some "talleres" or repair shops where cars are fixed. These are usually junky looking places with junk cars outside, tarpaper roofs and discarded parts lying all around. The typical auto repair shop in small Mexican towns is not concerned with esthetics…perhaps the junky appearance makes the shops easy to find without those flashing neon lights.

Of course you can always take your car or truck to the new car dealer in the city but you will pay dealer prices and there are many repair shortcuts dealers will not do. If you have a newer car and have say a drivability problem that requires testing equipment and perhaps electronic sensors you may end up having to go to the dealer anyway. But expect to pay.

Let me give an example of a series of repairs on my trusty old Toyota pickup.

The exhaust was making noise and like most drivers I put the repair off until the noise was just too loud. I could see the intermediate exhaust pipe was cracked and had a growing hole and was concerned that it might break and the catalytic converter would fall off, subsequently costing more money in the long run. I looked up the part on the internet and in Texas the part would run about 80 dollars and another 80-100 dollars for clamps and installation so the cost of the exhaust repair would run a bit less than 200 dollars. And considerably more if the catalytic converter fell off and cracked.

Not only that, the truck had begun to shake at around 10MPH and the shake had gotten progressively worse over time. I thought it was the transmission.

So I took it to my mechanic Manuel.

He took a blowtorch and cut off the end of the intermediate pipe and put a sleeve over the end of the pipe. Total cost was 200 pesos or about 16 dollars. We went for a ride to test the shake and since the muffler was fixed we could hear a squeaking noise at the rear of the truck as we took off. He crawled underneath and said one of the u-joints was bad. I asked him if it would make it to Texas and he shook his head. He showed me the play in the u-joint and a half hour later had the drive shaft out of the car.

But we had another problem. The bad u-joint had actually worn down part of the drive shaft and he said it would not be wise to simply put in a new u-joint. But he said the drive shaft could be fixed. We walked down the street, drive shaft in hand, to his welder friend who braised and welded the worn part for seven dollars. Miguel was satisfied so we went to the parts store to find the u-joint.

No luck. Manuel suggested we call AutoZone in the nearby city and fortunately they had the part. The next day we took the bus and bought the part at about 8 dollars. Plus the bus ride.

The following day we took the part to Manuel who put on the u-joint and reinstalled the driveshaft. We test drove the truck and shake was gone. The transmission was still good and I stopped thinking about buying another truck. So what might have been three or four hundred dollars in repairs in Texas ended up costing about 75 dollars in Mexico. Not quite as convenient, not quite as fast, but a good repair that lasted to Dallas and back.

Not all repair stories have such a happy ending. And not all mechanics are as honest and skilled as Manuel. What goes around comes around; since then I have sent Manuel a couple of new customers. If you need to find a good mechanic remember the mantra "ask, ask, ask."

But the point is you can get your car fixed in Mexico now and it's not like the old days when parts on "foreign" vehicles were not available. And if AutoZone does not have the part they will get it from Texas or California. It may take a little more time, but it is doable. Like Manuel says, "be patient and don't panic…all is possible."

And by the way, if you drive a Nissan, Volkswagen or Ford, parts are much more available. Toyotas and Hondas are now seen more often in Mexico but are still not common.

Another thought. Tires are more expensive in Mexico and tire quality on the average not as good so you may want to get tires before you cross into Mexico. And make sure you have a good spare. Mexican roads have more potholes and if you are like me, you will end up driving on many dirt and gravel roads so you want to have good tires.

And sorry for sounding like your father, but check your fluids regularly, change the oil, oil filter, fuel filter and air filter regularly as well. The dusty back roads sure take a toll. Oh, and don't forget the wiper blades. During the rainy season the Caribbean and Gulf coasts can have some real "frog strangler" rains and good wiper blades are a must.

Did I forget to mention to check your brakes?

22. Crossing the Mexican Border by Bus, Taxi or on Foot

If you travel alone, crossing the border by bus, taxi or walking is the cheapest way to enter Mexico. I have done it many times over the years, especially when I was younger and had little money.

One advantage of not going by car is all you need is a passport and your tourist visa to travel to the interior. Of course you have to get to the border but most major border crossings have numerous bus and taxi services available to help you get across. If you are at a smaller crossing you can even walk across.

You will need to stop by the immigration services to get your tourist visa.

Your bags may or may not be inspected upon entry. Then you proceed to the immigration office. Once you have your tourist permit, you can take a bus or more likely a taxi to the nearest bus station with bus service to the interior. Or you can stop off at a local hotel before proceeding south.

One advantage of taking an overnight bus is that you can sleep and not have to pay for a hotel room.

You will have to show your tourist permit and passport on the highway at the immigration checkpoint some 20 miles into the interior. You may have to take your bags from the baggage compartment for inspection. From that point on, you will probably not be inspected.

One real disadvantage of going by taxi and bus is you baggage is limited to what you can carry or drag. Using a backpack or rolling luggage will help but you will still find that lugging around luggage can be both tiring and limiting. Once you reach your destination you can unpack and all is well.

One consideration is what you will take. Start with the essentials and then with the desirables. Of course if you are crossing several times a year and have a place to store your gear you can take down different items on your return trips.

Most Mexicans travel by bus and so service is usually very good, regular and the better buses are comfortable with air conditioning, bathrooms and even movies. You may want to pick up some bottled water and sandwiches for the ride. Or perhaps a bag of candy to share with fellow travelers along the way. Sometimes the bus will make stops in larger towns and you will have time to get something to eat in the bus station. Just make sure you watch your valuables and get back on the bus on time.

Compared to the U.S., Mexican bus service is cheap but if you are going in a group such as your family you may want to pencil out a budget beforehand. You need to remember it is a long way from the border to many parts in the interior; get out your map and do some research before you go. It may cost you a hundred dollars or more to get where you are going.

Sometimes you will meet friendly and interesting people on the bus. Don't hesitate to strike up a conversation so you can practice your Spanish. Sometimes you can get some good pointers on travel and things to see and maybe make a new friend that will invite you for a visit.

In my younger years before I was married I always traveled alone and remember fondly the many good people I met traveling on the bus.

As your mother might have told you, now is not the time to be shy. Be careful, a bit wary, but also be friendly.

Y que te vayas bien!

23. Crossing the Mexican Border by Plane

Entering Mexico by plane is the quickest way to get to your destination but usually the most expensive. Then again, sometimes flying can be cheaper if you figure gas, hotels and meals when driving.

You can often save on plane fare by making reservations far in advance and staying longer. Also by avoiding peak travel times such as Christmas, spring break, Thanksgiving, etc. You should also look into peak travel times for Mexicans returning home for a visit, such as Easter week.

A very good way is to know your dates, or approximate dates, and use an Internet travel service such as Travelocity.com. By juggling your arrival and departure dates you can sometimes save quite a bit.

Another consideration is your destination. If you fly into Cancun on a Friday and return on a Sunday the rates can be higher. So plan and research well in advance. Also consider when you will return, you may not want to wait until the last day your tourist permit expires or return on Christmas Eve.

If you fly, the price of your tourist permit will be included in your airfare. The stewardess or steward will hand you a card to fill out an hour or so before landing. Fill out the card and carry it with you through immigration. Your bags will also be inspected and screened by X-ray as you pass through customs.

One disadvantage of air travel is you are physically limited as to what you can take. You may also find that excess weight and excess baggage can be quite expensive so it's a good idea to pack and weigh your bags well in advance and check with your carrier about additional baggage and excess weight fees. Put your packed suitcase on the bathroom scales to see how much it weighs. Then weigh yourself…no, just kidding…

Rental cars are now available at most major Mexican airports. You can check out rates and availabilities online. Rental cars are not really cheap but very convenient especially if your destination is a major city. You will need to check drop off sites in advance as extra fees will be added if your rental car is not returned to where you picked it up.

If you are more or less permanently retiring in Mexico you will want to return empty to the U.S. or almost empty except for gifts for friends and family. Keep a running list of what you need to bring on your return trip back to Mexico.

Do your research and you may find that flying is your best alternative depending where you leave from and return to. To be able to wake up in the jungles of Quintana Roo with the birds singing away and go to sleep that night in San Jose, California is simply amazing. We have made that trip many a time.

Flying is also so quick it can give you a "culture shock" especially if you have spent many months in Mexico. Funny thing about that culture shock, it goes both ways. May as well go try it out and see for yourself…

24. What Not to Take, What to Take and Returning Empty

As a tourist or turista, you are allowed to bring into Mexico personal items for your own use. The laws are common sense laws and you should use your common sense when preparing to enter Mexico.

There are certain restrictions that carry severe penalties. The most obvious are items that are expressly prohibited such as guns, ammunition and explosives. There are big signs at the border crossings that spell out these three items. Also prohibited are chemicals for manufacturing drugs, industrial equipment and more than $10,000 in cash.

But think about it. You are a retiree tourist, not a mercenary, illicit drug manufacturer, industrialist or money launderer. Common sense.

Also prohibited are new items in bulk, such as 100 new dresses, 100 new pairs of high heels or 100 pairs of new binoculars. Again, you are a retiree, not an importer.

Used items are much less scrutinized as are domestic and household items. A complete list of what is permitted and not permitted can be found by searching the government website.

For instance, you are allowed to bring a camera, laptop and pair of binoculars. These are personal items for your use and not for sale. If you drive, you may want to bring along some essential spare parts such as fuses and drive belts.

Importantly you should consider those essential items that you may not be able to get in Mexico. If you are under special medications, bring those as well as the prescriptions. If you have special needs, such as a cane, dentures or eyeglasses be sure to bring those. Again common sense.

One good way to start is to make a list of those items that are essential and start with those. Consider each item on its own. For instance, your toothbrush and toothpaste are essential items but they can be purchased in Mexico, for about the same price as in the United States. Let your good judgment, common sense and Mexican law be your guide.

You may have some items that you would like to take but do not have the room. You can store and save those items to bring on subsequent trips.

It is a good idea during your stay to keep a list of what you need and cannot find in Mexico, or perhaps it is prohibitively expensive. If you return to the U.S. “empty” you can bring those items with you on your return.

There are services in larger American cities such as Houston or San Diego that will carry packages to Mexican destinations. These tend to service limited areas in Mexico and are expensive. Common carriers such as UPS and DHL also provide service to Mexico but rates are also expensive.

There is no charge, tax or duty to tourists for bringing in your personal belongings. Once again, as you can see the Mexican government is doing all it can to make you welcome in Mexico.

25. Pets

If you don't want to go through the hassle and expense of bringing a pet from the U.S. into Mexico, you can buy a pet in Mexico. Many pets are for sale though many also come from the notorious "puppy farms". Scotty came to us a stray and just kept staying. Of course when you go back north to renew your papers you will have to make plans for your pet's care.

Many cats and dogs in Mexico are feral, strays or "street" animals. Even though these animals have "owners", they are allowed to roam the streets and may be gone days at a time. Many owners are irresponsible and do not provide proper care for their pets but that is also true of the United States.

We have also met many pet owners who are very conscientious about their pets.

If you have a cat or dog that is a member of your family and you drive, you will want to take them with you to Mexico.

Technically speaking, you are supposed to have an official "Certificate of Veterinary Inspection Companion Animal" which includes a destination. Just have the vet put where you plan to go in Mexico.

An inspection or exam costs about $50 which includes the transport certificate. We did the inspection for the first trip and have only been asked if we had dog papers one time. Usually the Mexican customs officials will not ask for pet papers.

It is a good idea to keep all your pet's papers in a "Pet Papers" folder including a history of all shots. Your dog should have a current shots of rabies, parvo, distemper, corona virus, etc. Like humans, it's better to be on the safe side then take the risk your dog will get sick.

Heartworm is a malady to be avoided. Be sure to give heartworm medicine to your dog at least every two months. Heartguard is the most common brand and is available at pet stores in Mexico. Heartworm is spread by mosquitoes and is preventable and your dog will be exposed to mosquitoes in Mexico.

Unlike the U.S., heartworm medication is available in Mexico over the counter and does not require a vet's prescription.

You can also get shots at veterinary offices in Mexico. We do it on both sides of the border just to make sure so there will be no problems either entering Mexico or returning to the U.S. We give our dogs a "generic" shot once a year in Mexico that costs about $15 U.S.

We have never been asked for pet papers upon reentering the U.S.; only comments from the customs official such as "is the dog American too?"

Vets and larger supermarkets carry pet foods many of which have a familiar American label. In the past most owners gave their dogs table scraps but now many owners are using dog food. You can get a large bag in the supermarket or many vet and pet shops sell dry dog feed for about $2 U.S. per kilo or 2.2 pounds.

You should check the official government requirements for pets before taking your pet into Mexico. It would be unfortunate to spoil your trip simply because you lacked some paperwork such as proof of a rabies shot. A simple web search will give you the necessary information.

You should also take a leash and a chain in case you are in areas where you need to have your dog tied.

A large number of other types of pets are permitted in Mexico including hamsters and turtles. Numbers are limited so you cannot take in 50 rabbits even if they give birth while crossing the bridge.

If you drive, you should keep your pet's papers in your dash. Sometimes the municipal police will ask to see your dog papers. You will probably be okay but it's better to have the papers with you to avoid paying a "mordida."

And be considerate of your dog in the heat. As the temperature can soar along with the humidity, a pet in a closed vehicle can die very quickly. Either roll the windows down or take your pet with you. I have even had children nearby to watch my dog while we eat in a restaurant.

And don't forget the water bottle. Pets exposed to heat will consume much more water and we always keep several liters in plastic bottles just in case. If you forget you can always buy bottled water at corner grocery store.

If your dog is prone to fleas, it's best to give the dog a good bath with a flea soap once a week. Leave the soap on the dog for 15-20 minutes before rinsing. Fleas lay eggs that can all of the sudden hatch and cause problems. Stray cats also are a constant source of fleas so be prepared. Any vet or pet store will have flea soap.

And don't forget check for those pesky ticks and pinollillos. We check every few days as ticks can be found anywhere there is brush or grass and especially around cattle.

You should also keep close watch on your pet and keep them away from potential thieves. Thieves will steal your pet and then resell them or extort money from you for their return.

There you have it. Not the final word by any means but don't forget to plan for your pet when you retire and visit Mexico. As a member of your family you will want to make sure their papers are in order and their needs met. If the situation were reversed, they would do the same for you, no?

26. National (Internal) Travel by Plane, Rental Car, Bus and Taxi

Internal flights within Mexico are restricted to Mexican carriers and are not open to outside competition. When Mexicana Airlines when bankrupt several years ago, it left Aeromexico as the principle national carrier with essentially a national monopoly. Aeromexico immediately raised its fares sometimes by as much as twice the old fares.

Consequently internal flights within Mexico are expensive, limited to major cities and by U.S. standards not frequent. A new airline, Airbus, is trying to make inroads but flights are few and service limited and complaint ridden. Check internet travel sites for schedules and fares.

Rental cars are another mode of travel but are restricted to major cities and airports. Fees tend to be expensive, in the $60-90 U.S. per day range. Additional fees are charged for not returning vehicles to the point of origin. When you pick up your vehicle be sure to have the agency employees note on your paperwork any damages on your rental vehicle such as dents or scratches. You can reserve rental cars via the internet.

Bus is the most common mode of travel within Mexico. There are essentially three levels or classes of bus service.

First class buses are modern, clean, air conditioned and almost always on time. Round trip and one way tickets can be purchased in advance which is advisable, especially during peak travel periods. First class busses are usually direct and do not make unscheduled stops.

If you are traveling long distances, such as to border cities, first class travel is the way to go. Arrivals and departures are limited to major bus terminals in larger cities. Most schedules and reservations are available online. ADO is the major company providing first class bus service.

Second class bus service is almost as good and a bit cheaper. Buses do stop in smaller cities and towns but might not stop along the highways.

Third class buses are older, without air conditioning, make frequent stops along the route, take much longer and are much cheaper, usually less than 50% cheaper than first class buses. Baggage is not restricted and you will find locals carrying chickens and turkeys and large boxes. Reservations and advanced tickets are not available but during certain times seats are not available and you will have to stand.

Taxi service is of two varieties. The first is a standard type of service where you flag down the taxi and they take you where you want to go. It is always a good idea to ask up front what the charge will be.

The second type of service is a "sitio" or site service that is fixed. The taxi will take you from one site to another site, either in the same town or city or to a nearby town. Taxis line up at the sites and will fill up with passengers before they leave; sometimes taking as many as 6-8 people. Fares are fixed and are relatively cheap but you do go crammed together. These taxis will usually make stops if you want to get out along the way.

In larger towns and in cities you will usually have multiple taxi and bus options so it is a good idea to inquire and learn about service availability. One way to explore a new city is to take a bus or taxi ride out and walk back to your hotel room or apartment.

As you become familiar with these forms of public transit you may find them more convenient than driving since in many cities and larger towns parking can be a problem.

Public transportation in general is much better than in the United States. Learn to use it and your life will be much easier.

27. Budgeting, "No Spend Days" and Living Modestly but Well

Budgeting means knowing how much you have and when and how much you need to spend. This means that you will have enough money to cover your necessary expenses with some left over for extra expenses, savings, "rainy day" expenses, travel back home, unexpected expenses, spur of the moment spending decisions, etc.

Having a good budget means you will always have enough money to live, perhaps even live well with enough left over for other things.

One simple way to figure out your budget is to take your monthly income and divide it by 30 giving you the amount you have to spend each day. So if you have a 1200 dollars a month in income, or about 15,000 pesos, that leaves you about 500 pesos a day or 3500 pesos a week to spend.

If your rent and utilities are 3000 pesos a month, that leaves you with 12000 pesos a month for food, transportation, incidentals, etc., or about 400 pesos a day or 2800 pesos a week. A little over 200 dollars a week.

To refine your budget, you should take out your 180 day return to the border travel expenses; air fare, bus, hotel, meals, etc.

But the daily, weekly, monthly figure is a good way to get an idea of how much you really have to spend compared to how much you would like to spend.

So let's say you go to Chedraui, Soriana or Wal-Mart and spend 1000 pesos, which is maybe three or four big bags of groceries. You will find that is not hard to do, especially as you arrive and stock your kitchen with oil, sugar, coffee, tea, oatmeal, raisins, flour, toilet paper, etc. If your budget is 400 pesos a day, you will have exceeded several days budget. So now you need to make amends.

Take a day or two where you spend no money, except for maybe tortillas and local bus fare. Prepare your own food, eat what you have bought, take walks, go to the free museums, visit friends, etc. It's not hard to do and it puts you right back on budget.

Of course the same general principles of frugal, simple living that apply to Mexico apply as well to any other country. Waste not, buy specials and in bulk, eat what is in season, freeze what you can't eat today, don't eat out every meal, turn off the fan when not in use, take the bus instead of a taxi, etc. Living simply and frugally is much easier when you have the time; you can walk to the store, search for bargains, eat with friends, cook, etc.

If you think your budget is too much on a "shoestring", consider that it will cost twice as much to live in the US and that the average Mexican worker earns less than 1000 pesos a week. Over half of the Mexican population lives in poverty yet they find ways to make do. They have to. There are no food stamps in Mexico. And the odds are if you are a poor Mexican your relatives are also poor so they can't help you out.

There are only two ways to save more: earn more and spend less. Since you are retired and not looking to work, you can put your focus on spending less.

And living simply does not mean you can't live well. You may in fact decide that doing more with less is the most sensible way to live.

As a general rule, I have found that most luxury products and services are to a certain extent a waste, with more flash and presumption than value. Evaluate what you buy, especially the higher ticket items, and see if you really need it.

Besides, it's just not common sense to have a champagne lifestyle on a beer budget, no?

28. Best Quality of Life at the Best Price

If we return back to your requirements and budget matrix, we can conclude that the best strategy is one that allows for the best quality of life at the best price.

How you determine your quality of life is specific to your needs, wants and resources. In general, we can define the quality of life as being able to do what you want, when you want to do it and feeling satisfied about the result. We can also add that having the time or free time to do what you want is paramount, and that is what quality of life is all about.

When we are able to do what we want we are said to "be in the flow".

One way to assess the requirements for your optimized quality of life is to look at the extremes or perhaps the best case and worst case scenarios of each of your major expenses. Are there other options or alternatives?

Let's say you live in a colonia just outside of Puerto Vallarta, need to go back to the U.S. to renew your papers which you normally do by flying to San Francisco, really want to take the train ride from Los Mochis to visit the Copper Canyon and have a cousin in El Paso that wants you to come for a visit.

So instead of spending $1100 on plane fare and expenses from Vallarta to SFO, you take the bus to Los Mochis, the train to Creel, stop off for a side trip to Batopilas, return to the train and go to Cuauhtémoc and Chihuahua and then take the bus from Chihuahua to Juarez, a taxi to the Chamizal bridge where you cancel your tourist permit and your cousin picks you up. On your return trip you take the bus from Juarez to Vallarta. Total cost is $900 plus you got your dream side trip to Tarahumara land and the Copper Canyon.

You did what you wanted to do and at less cost.

Let's look at another example with rent. In Vallarta you are renting a small one bedroom apartment for 4500 pesos a month. Yet you find yourself alone with lots of free time and you are not satisfied that you are learning Spanish at a pace that you think you could.

As an alternative, you find a rental room with a family in a working class neighborhood that includes dinner for 3500 pesos a month. You pay cheaper rent, get your dinners included, eat with a Mexican family that immerses you nightly in Spanish, make new friends, housesit when the family goes to visit relatives and even babysit the kids when the parents have to go out at night.

Once again, you ended up doing what you wanted to do when you wanted to do it at a more efficient cost. And improved the quality of your life.

You can do the same with all of your expenses once you have settled in. You may even find opportunities that will come your way that you did not expect.

These are just a few examples but hopefully you get the pictorial concept. Use your requirements budget matrix to optimize your quality of life and then refine it as time goes by.

It's a good, smart, adventuresome way to live and realize your Mexican dream.

29. Pesos, Dollars, Exchange Rates, ATMs and Banking

The peso is the national currency of Mexico. Coins or "monedas" are sometimes found in 10 centavos and 50 centavos or cents of a peso but more commonly coins are one peso, two pesos, five pesos and ten pesos. Bills are of 20, 50, 100, 200, 500 and 1000 peso notes. You should familiarize yourself with all of these coins and bills.

In some tourist areas, such as Cancun and Acapulco, dollars can be used as currency in lieu of pesos. Most border towns, on both sides of the border, accept both pesos and dollars as standard currency.

The exchange rate is the number of pesos that are the monetary equivalent of one dollar. In recent years, the exchange rate has fluctuated between 12 and 14 to the dollar. Money can be exchanged at banks or "casas de cambio", money exchange houses. Sometimes banks may limit the amount you can exchange and sometimes they will require your passport to register you according to the recent anti money-laundering laws.

Obviously once you have settled down you should go to the place that gives you the best exchange rate and occasionally monitor the exchange rates at local banks and "casas de cambio". The difference may not be much, but when you are living on a fixed income and limited budget every bit helps.

You will now find ATMs in most towns throughout Mexico. ATMs are also found in most large supermarkets such as Soriana, Chedraui, Wal-Mart and Costco. You can currently withdraw up to 5,000 pesos per day at an ATM. This means that you can have your pension or social security directly deposited in your bank account in the U.S. and with your debit card make a withdrawal in pesos in Mexico.

The advantages are you do not have to open a bank account in Mexico and you do not have to carry around large amounts of cash wherever you go. The instructions for cash withdrawals are also in English and are straightforward, basically the same as in the U.S. Don't forget your PIN number!

For security reasons, sometimes you may be denied access to funds by your bank in the U.S. so before you leave on your trip you may want to call them and tell them you will be traveling in Mexico. If you are denied funds, you will have to call them anyway before you can access cash withdrawals.

A few thoughts on ATM withdrawals in Mexico. Exercise caution when making a withdrawal just as you would in the U.S. You will be asked when making a withdrawal to authorize a transfer fee that may be 40-70 pesos or roughly five American dollars. You must approve this charge and the charge is the same if you withdraw any amount. At five dollars a pop you may want to plan your withdrawals and make larger withdrawal amounts to save on fee surcharges.

You should also look at the exchange rate or the amount of pesos you get per peso with an ATM withdrawal. This may vary slightly from day to day or in slightly more in more "unstable" economic periods. Most rates are pretty honest but if you find a particular ATM company or bank is not giving you a good exchange rate, do not use them.

You should always request a receipt for your records. As you can see you can have ready access to direct deposits to your U.S. checking account, such as pension and social security deposits.

As for opening a bank account in Mexico, you will undoubtedly hear horror stories of extra fees, limited access to funds, etc. so I will not recommend you open a bank account. I have also heard of many folks, including myself, that have had no problems at all. Ask the locals where you settle for their opinions.

You can also send or receive money sent from the U.S. to Mexico and vice-versa. Western Union and other services will charge a fee for the service, usually a set fee, for sending up to a maximum amount. Check with these companies to find out more details.

One other comment on money. When you cross into Mexico, you should have some pesos available. When you cross back into the U.S., you should have some dollars. On both sides of the border there will be stores that do not accept both currencies and the further from the border you get the more this practice is found. So save those extra pesos or dollars for your return trip.

So there you have a thumbnail sketch of the all-important topic money. Do your homework, learn the do's and don'ts and mind your dollars and pesos!

30. Working, Earning Money and Bartering

Strictly speaking, it is illegal to work in Mexico without a work visa. If you are caught, you could be deported and possibly denied reentry. Practically speaking, this only applies to legitimate, full time jobs and there are certainly some gray areas.

However, if you are in doubt about your working status, you should inquire and possibly apply for a work visa.

This does not apply however if you work for yourself, such as a photographer or painter or graphic designer and do not sell your work in Mexico. Many self-employed individuals work and live in Mexico and sell their wares elsewhere.

For instance, if you were to privately tutor a group of students in English you most likely would not be prosecuted. But if you were to open an English school available to the public you would be at possible risk. Once again, you should do an internet search of the government to see the latest restrictions.

There is also a special category of consultant and advisor that does not require a formal work visa since you are not technically an employee. Once again, consult the official government websites.

Bartering is another matter as no monetary exchange is involved. If you were to trade English lessons for a reduction in your rent, then that would probably not be a problem.

In general, Mexico is not the place to go if you are poor or don't have the means to support yourself. You can live on a small pension but it is hard to earn money in a country where half the population lives in poverty, small businesses are marginally profitable and open employment will put your tourist status at risk.

This does not mean that if you hustle a little bit and do it discreetly, you will be in jeopardy. Mexico is a country where many millions of people have to hustle on some level just to survive.

Use your common sense and good judgment. Ask those that you know for their opinion. Never say never but always tread lightly.

Like Ben Franklin once said, there are two ways to save money; earn more and spend less. Since in Mexico it will be hard to earn money, put your focus and effort on spending less. And spending wisely.

One final point -- ask, ask, ask. Do not hesitate to ask your friends, neighbors and even strangers where to buy something or get something cheaper. Most Mexicans have to make ends meet with a lot less money than a tourist does so they are ready made "experts" to living simply and "thriftily."

Just because you are a tourist does not mean you have to be pretentious and act like one. Just kidding…

31. Speaking Spanish

Retiring, living and traveling in Mexico will give you a unique opportunity to learn to speak Spanish. Spanish is the national language of Mexico and although many people speak some English, you will find that outside of the tourist zones very few people actually speak English well.

Necessity is the mother of invention because necessity provides a motivation that cannot be duplicated in any other way. If everyone around you is speaking Spanish then you cannot help but learn some Spanish; the level you attain depends on your attitude, motivation and willingness.

You already have learned one language and there is no reason you cannot learn another.

Without a doubt, the best way to learn another language is to be "immersed" in a situation where that language is spoken. For that reason, foreign students pay to live with a family, take lessons in Spanish and become immersed in it. You don't have to pay any extra for the opportunity; it comes with the territory when you decide to live in Mexico.

If you took some Spanish in high school or college then you are already one step ahead. What you learned will quickly come back to you. If you have never taken a Spanish class you can sign up for one at your local junior college or adult education center before you come.

There are also many short course and reference websites on the internet. Check them out.

It will help to get a good pocket dictionary that you can carry in your purse or back pocket. Refer to it often throughout your day. You can also buy many books and language CD's (including mine!) that will help serve as a guide. As you come across words in your activities of daily living, learn them. Own them. Make them become yours.

There are maybe a hundred words that are used 70% of the time. Make sure those words become your linguistic "property."

A good way to rapidly increase your vocabulary is by buying the newspaper in Spanish; if not every day at least several times a week and especially on Sundays. I learned basic Spanish when I was in Spain by going to the coffee shops, buying a newspaper and pulling out my pocket dictionary when I came across common words.

It is important to learn correct grammar as grammar and syntax are essential to speaking Spanish well. But don't dwell exclusively on just grammar. Try to speak Spanish whenever you get the chance. Communicating effectively in Spanish with those around you provides a great deal of positive reinforcement and satisfaction which will further stimulate your motivation.

There are two general strategies that will help you in your quest: developing an ear for Spanish and learning to speak with a correct accent.

By listening constantly to spoken Spanish you will develop your ear for it and over time begin to distinguish different sounds. This is critical for increasing your comprehension. If you are in the United States, listen to Spanish language radio and listen to TV programs such as the news in Spanish. All major U.S. cities now have Spanish language radio and TV stations.

The other key strategy is to speak Spanish whenever you have the opportunity. Practice, practice, practice. The more you practice the better you develop your skills.

You cannot expect everyone to speak English with you in Mexico, even if you live in a tourist area. Most Mexicans will appreciate your efforts to learn Spanish and many will be glad to give you a little help.

One other consideration. Do not become too self-conscious. People may at times snicker at your inability but that is part of the learning process. Do not take it personally, laugh with them, shrug it off and proceed ahead with as much intensity as you can.

In six months you should have a basic vocabulary of 1500-2500 words. This will allow you to carry out your activities of daily living, get directions, buy food at the markets, understand prices and change, etc. The more you learn the richer your experience.

If you live in Mexico for several years and study and practice on a daily basis and immerse yourself communicating with the local population, you should reach a level of basic fluency.

You can gauge your progress by the amount of translation or mental translation you need to do to understand. When you get to the point where you don't have to translate in your head and can express yourself without translating each word, you have arrived. Or are arriving. You will be surprised at the degree of personal satisfaction this will give you.

It takes time, effort and practice. You can't do it in a week or two but you can make steady progress if you keep focused on your goal, don't get frustrated, practice speaking whenever you can and don't become overly self-conscious.

If others, including little children, can do it, so can you!

32. Idioms, Usage, Rhythms, Accents and Foul Language

Spoken Spanish across Mexico is not uniform. There are regional differences sometimes within very short distances. Additionally many Indigenous dialects and languages exist that are freely mixed with Spanish. One afternoon I found it interesting to listen the taxi drivers in Coba, a Maya ruin on the Yucatan, speak Spanish and Maya with a 50-50 mix.

With these regional differences are a plethora of idioms or word usages that have specific meanings in the areas they are spoken and do not follow the normal grammar and syntax of more formal Spanish. For instance, to drink alcohol may be tomar, beber, chupar, etc. depending on where you are located. In Campeche State, the word chumar is used. Someone that is drunk may not be “borracho” but “chumado“.

While creating a vast linguistic and cultural richness, the use of idioms does present a problem with the beginning student of Spanish. While a resident of Merida may understand what ‘borracho’ means, the beginning student of Spanish such as yourself may not understand what ‘chumado’ means.

You can only do your best and try at least initially, to learn the correct way of speaking that is accepted throughout Mexico.

Another variation in spoken Spanish is rhythm or pace at which Spanish is spoken. Residents of Mexico City, now commonly known as Chilangos, have an unmistakably sing song rhythmic way of speaking. Once you clearly hear this rhythm you can immediately determine the speaker is from the Distrito Federal or Mexico City.

Accents also vary from region and even within the same state. This is why it is important to develop your ear for Spanish; once you have a well-developed ear you can understand what is being said with different accents.

I still after many years have some difficulties understanding the Spanish spoken by the Campechanos from Campeche on the Yucatan peninsula. Not only do they speak extremely fast but they mix multiple idioms, many of Maya origin, with a strong regional accent. Such is language and such is life. Live with it and try to do your best.

You will also hear in certain regions, such as the Gulf Coast, generous usage of foul and obscene language. What might be surprising is that young children and elderly women freely use these obscenities and it might make you a bit uncomfortable sitting around the dinner table listening to a steady stream of cursing.

You will find mixed opinions of why this is and what should or should not be done about it.

My opinion is that if it is common usage or the vernacular that is different and more acceptable even for young children and elderly ladies. Many Mexicans, including my dear wife, strongly disagree. They say an obscenity is an obscenity no matter in what context, vernacular or usage it is used. You will probably form your own opinion as well. Once again, it is what it is.

Then of course there are the Spaniards, Cubans, Puerto Ricans, Chileans and others that feel their Spanish is superior but I don't concern myself with these differences. One tends to think that one's own language and culture is superior and that is just how people feel.

All you can do is your best and forge ahead…

33. The Mental Benefits of Learning a New Language and Culture

As we age, we begin to worry about memory loss, dementia, senile dementia and Alzheimer's. To date there are no "cures" for these maladies; no medications or vitamins that cure or realistically even lessen the effects.

However, one "cure" or way to lessen symptoms is to use the brain in new or novel ways.

What has been clinically shown is that learning a new language, a new culture or essentially anything new will help prevent and forestall the negative mental consequences of aging. On an almost monthly basis new scientific and medical studies are showing the benefits of continuous learning for the aged, aging and elderly…as well as everyone else.

This has been specifically shown for learning a new language. Learning a new language creates positive brain plasticity or growth of brain tissue creating new connections between neurons. It is also thought that new neural channels or pathways are created though research in this field is just beginning to be developed.

Learning a new language makes you develop and use new linguistic tools. And if you are fortunate enough to be in an immersion situation where all that surrounds you is new, you will be "forced" to learn.

At this point we need not concern ourselves with the specifics of the research but a simple internet search will reveal this trend. What we do know that learning a new language is one of the best things you can do for yourself whether young or old.

This is another reason why you should not retire to Mexico and live in an enclave where you are seldom exposed to Spanish and Mexican culture. If you do isolate yourself you will not be able to access this opportunity and the corresponding benefits.

Many retirees worry first about will they have enough money to retire and then worry about having something to do. By not having anything "to do" retirees can become frustrated or even depressed with their new lifestyle.

Learning a new language, Spanish, and learning a new culture, Mexican will keep you busy for many years. I have been living and traveling in Mexico off and on for over 40 years and I learn something new every day. It has not only enriched my life but has always given me something to do; I do not seem to ever get bored in Mexico.

Of course you must be thinking you are not like me and it may not work the same for you. Well, in part you may be right. But at any level, even at a superficial level, you can receive many benefits from speaking Spanish and learning about Mexican culture.

And if you are going to retire, live and travel in Mexico, why not take advantage of this unique opportunity?

34. Dental Care

Many Americans go to Mexico for dental care as it can be from 50% to 80% cheaper for the equivalent care found in the United States. While this may be true, it is also true that some care may be substandard by U.S. standards so one should be careful when choosing a dentist.

Mexicans have a different view of dental care than Americans. Dental care is often not considered at all until teeth become a problem. As a consequence, many Mexicans lose all their teeth by the time they are 50 and require dentures. For many Mexican dentists and their patients, if a tooth becomes a problem the only solution is to have it removed.

That is why many middle-aged Mexicans will have missing front teeth and gold or silver crowns. The perception is that colored crowns and caps are not ugly and are very common among poor and lower middle class Mexicans. Affluent Mexicans spend whatever is necessary on whitened teeth and braces.

There is essentially no dental insurance in Mexico and government sponsored dental programs for the poor are both inadequate and cost driven, meaning that teeth are often removed as a quick alternative.

Since we live in Mexico, we have been forced to find local dentists at each of our home bases and the difference in the quality of care is significant.

As usual you get what you pay for. Once again; ask, ask, ask. See what others recommend and try out a dentist first to determine the level of care they provide. You can start by having a general cleaning. This is a service that many Mexicans never have and never consider having. The idea is why spend good money on teeth that don't hurt and are not loose?

From a cleaning you can determine many things about a dentist. We have been to low quality dentists and simply do not return. For instance, if a dentist cleans your teeth and does not clean between your teeth, then their fees may be cheap but the care is also cheap. And for many of us in our mature years, adequate dental care is not optional.

For a good cleaning, we pay 300-400 pesos or $25-30 U.S. This is about twice what a cheap cleaning would normally cost with other dentists but is much more thorough and still at about 25% of what a similar service would cost in the U.S. Cavities and filling "rebuilds" can cost from 500-800 pesos depending on the work involved.

While these fees seem inexpensive to Americans they are expensive for most Mexicans. If you have gum problems like I do, in Mexico you can afford to have cleanings three or four times a year as opposed to twice yearly in the U.S.

My dentist spent two hours working on one of my teeth to save it. That was six months ago and so far so good. It cost me about $60. Equivalent dental work in California would have cost me $1000. My wife has had several teeth that have been saved by our dentist whose fees are more than most local dentists, but clearly worth it.

I once had a toothache that got progressively worse and finally had to go to the dentist. After working on the tooth for fifteen minutes she found a raspberry seed stuck down deep in my gum. Needless to say I now avoid fruit with smaller seeds or extract the seeds first. An unscrupulous dentist would have recommended an unnecessary procedure.

A good dentist will also do several things that are indicators of their professionalism. One is the use of X-rays. Before drilling out for an extensive cavity, our dentist takes an x-ray to determine the nature of the cavity. She charges for the x-ray but considers an x-ray necessary for good care. Also when more extensive work is required, she refers us to an oral surgeon or orthodontist.

Many Americans go to Mexico for dentures which can be considerably less expensive than in the U.S. The average set of dentures will cost from $300-400 U.S. or slightly more. This may be as little as 5-10% of what comparable dentures will cost in the U.S. I have seen dentures that fit perfectly and dentures that did not fit well at all. Ill-fitting dentures may be cheaper but come with an unacceptable trade-off. Once again, ask, ask, ask.

Dental care is much more expensive in tourist areas, big cities and border cities. Also be wary of dentists that suggest you should have all or most of your teeth pulled and replaced with dentures. These dentists are charlatans. All teeth should be saved if possible, even as you enter your advanced years. Your dental mantra should be "save what can be saved."

Toothpaste, toothbrushes and floss are readily available in most supermarkets and are inexpensive.

In summary, when seeking dental care ask around for the best dentists locally even if they are considered to be "too expensive" by the locals. Try out one and if you are happy with their service, stick with them.

In the end you have to ask yourself the simple question, "what are my teeth worth?”

35. Health Care

Many Americans look to Mexico for health care they cannot afford in the United States. As you will find with many aspects of life in Mexico, there are both advantages and disadvantages.

In general, medical costs are much lower than in the United States. Sometimes the quality is not as good and sometimes it is. Also many services and procedures are not available in Mexico or available only in large metropolitan areas.

Standard medical practice in Mexico is also different. Treatment is usually more aggressive "up front" with fewer tests, analyses, follow up visits and hospitalizations. Straightforward maladies such as sore throats and bronchitis are treated aggressively with powerful antibiotics.

This means that you may get better faster but side effects, reactions and complications can be problematic. There are clear medical arguments on both sides and you will have to decide what is in your best interest by using your common sense. In general you as a patient have to accept more responsibility for your care, which once again can be a plus or a minus.

There are three basic types of government care in Mexico; care for government workers, workers covered under a social security system and a nationalized care plan called "Seguro Popular" for those that have no other medical coverage. You may not have access to these hospitals and clinics unless you are covered under one of these plans.

However, there are problems with these services and many patients complain of poor service, lack of procedures, lack of medicines, etc. As a consequence many patients that are covered under these plans opt for private care first.

As a tourist you will almost certainly seek care in the private medical sector unless you have a medical emergency.

Doctors in private practice charge lower fees than in the U.S. usually in the range of $12-25 U.S. per visit depending on their specialty. Mexico is a relatively poor country and most Mexicans cannot afford high medical fees so doctors have to price accordingly.

Unless you have a specific problem requiring a specialist you can see a general practitioner. My experience is that most are competent; you come in with a simple medical problem, they speak with you and possibly give you an examination and they write you a prescription. For 90% of your medical needs this will suffice.

If you have a brain tumor, a complicated heart problem or require extensive surgery the situation changes. You will have to seek out specialists in larger Mexican cities or return to the U.S. for care.

Always ask for referrals from the locals. In general, Mexico has good medical care available at much more reasonable prices than in the U.S.

36. Drugs: Prescription and Otherwise

Prescription drugs are readily available in pharmacies throughout Mexico in all cities and many larger towns. Some specific drugs may not be available in all pharmacies so if you are taking specific drugs you may want to bring along an extra supply as well as your prescription.

Most prescription drugs are cheaper than in the U.S. with some drugs being considerably cheaper.

Gone are the days when tourists cross the border to buy massive amounts of prescription drugs over the counter in large quantities. Such purchases in many cases are also illegal to carry back when returning the U.S.

Gone too are the days when antibiotics, amphetamines, diet pills and antidepressant drugs could be bought over the counter without a prescription. You will need to check which drugs you can purchase without a prescription and since neither my wife nor I take any medications, at least for now, I can't really give you any pointers.

Some pharmacies have a doctor "on staff" or readily available that will write you a prescription for a nominal fee, sometimes as little as 30 pesos or $2.50 U.S. If say you have a sore throat, you go the pharmacy, the doctor speaks with you, may or may not look at your throat and then write you a prescription for an antibiotic.

Some pharmacies will require that you see a doctor first for a prescription.

In general Mexican medicine and the Mexican public in general, are "medicine driven", that is, every illness has a medication cure. Other forms of treatment are much less common as is prevention.

So if a Mexican drinks cokes three times a day and develops diabetes, they are given an insulin prescription and told to cut back on the cokes. Incidentally, Mexicans have the highest consumption of soft drinks in the world as well as one of the world's highest diabetes rates.

Ideally if you have a medical problem you should see a doctor first for a consultation.

As for illegal drugs, they are readily available in all urban areas and larger towns. Since neither of us do illegal drugs, I can't give you many specifics on the subject.

If you do illegal drugs, there are a few points to consider. For possession of larger quantities of illegal drugs you can go to prison, certainly not a pleasant prospect in Mexico. For smaller quantities, you will probably be able to get off with a fine and/or warning, something you should avoid so you don't jeopardize your tourist status.

No matter what, if you are caught with illegal drugs it can be quite a hassle. Remember that your passport number and tourist permit number are logged into a national database and you do not want black marks appearing when you try to reenter Mexico.

Socially, if you consume illegal drugs you will be considered a drug user, whether you smoke pot or inject heroin. It may not seem just, since you can get stinking drunk on tequila, fight and cause all kinds of problems and still not be stigmatized as much as if you smoke an occasional joint.

Mexico is not California or Colorado. You will rarely go to a social function where recreational drugs are used.

Once again, be smart and use your common sense. And go real easy on the tequila...

37. Dengue and Mosquitoes

The good news is Mexico is now officially malaria free; the bad news is that dengue fever is a growing health menace. I had a "mild" case of dengue and believe me you want to take all possible precautions to avoid contracting it.

Dengue is a virus spread by mosquitoes. A mosquito bites a person infected with dengue and then spreads the virus by biting another person. Subsequently dengue can be more prevalent in areas that are populated since the greater the population the greater the likelihood that someone will have dengue.

Dengue is primarily found in tropical and subtropical areas but has now spread to other areas as well. Any place that has mosquitoes can also have dengue. Dengue also is more prevalent in the summer and fall months.

The dengue virus effects the blood and specifically the blood platelet count. There is no cure and there is no vaccine. In fact, taking pain relievers such as aspirin or Tylenol can be counterproductive.

The symptoms of dengue are fever, chills, no appetite and general weakness. Many dengue sufferers complain of severe pain located behind the eyeballs.

There are three classifications of dengue.

The first is dengue "light" or a moderate case. This is what I had; fever and chills for about a week and a generalized weakness for another three weeks. Total down time is about a month.

The second category is classical dengue or "dengue classico". Fever and chills may last for a month or more with general weakness lasting several more months. Total down time is around three months.

The third category is hemorrhagic dengue or "dengue hemoragico." This is the most severe form of dengue and in extreme cases can result in death. Symptoms are ongoing fever and chills, severe headaches, loss of appetite and bleeding through the nose and sometimes the mouth. Treatment requires hospitalization and often blood transfusions to increase platelet counts. Total down time is six months or more.

If you think you have dengue and are in a dengue area, see a doctor as soon as possible. You will be examined and be requested to get a blood analysis. Diagnosis is almost always determined by a low platelet count.

Several important points. The healthier you are and the better diet you have, the better you will be able to resist the dengue virus. Recovery from dengue requires rest and more rest as the body fights off the virus. Recovery may also involve purple areas developing on the feet and moving up the legs. This is normal but also a bit spooky.

The best prevention of dengue is to prevent being bitten by mosquitoes.

Bring a good flyswatter with you when you come. Also bring a good repellent such as "Repel" from the U.S. Make sure your room has screens and keep the door closed using air conditioning or a fan to stay cool. If your room doesn't have adequate screens use a mosquito net when you sleep. There are good ones in the U.S. You can buy one to bring with you -- they can be folded taking up little space and weigh very little.

Each night before going to sleep take your trusty flyswatter and kill all the mosquitoes you find.

Avoid going outside in mosquito prone areas at dawn and dusk as these are the times when mosquitoes tend to swarm.

As a foreigner you will have less natural immunity to dengue than the locals and "natives". Do everything you can to avoid being bitten. Odds are you will never contract the dengue virus but you want to keep the odds in your favor.

Dengue is serious business. You shouldn't be scared but you should be wary. Forewarned is forearmed.

38. Dysentery, "Turista" and Montezuma's Revenge

Ah, the "turista"! Montezuma was of course an Aztec emperor during Cortez' conquest of Mexico. So the term revenge is used as a humorous sarcasm to those foreigner's that come to visit Mexico.

But of course it actually isn't a form of revenge.

It has to do with the stomach and intestines we humans carry around inside us. Inside our gastrointestinal tract are multitudes of bacteria that reside there and help us process our food and eliminate our waste. It may not be glamorous but that is the way we as animals are put together and function.

When we live in a certain area we eat the food and drink the water of that area and consequently absorb the bacteria of that area. When we physically change areas we change the bacteria and sometimes the body will react by giving us stomach pains, diarrhea and fever with chills.

This not only happens when Americans go to Mexico but also when Mexicans go to America.

If you go to Mexico for a week or two you can avoid the "turista" by drinking only bottled water and being very careful about the food you eat. If you retire, live and travel in Mexico this is simply not practical. If you eat the food and drink the water, sooner or later your body will adjust and you will get "the runs."

As a general rule, the further away you go from the border the more severe the dysentery. For instance, in Vera Cruz you may get the "turista" for a day and then it is gone. If you go to the U.S. and return on a regular basis you most likely will only have a good (or bad) case of the "turista" only once.

However, if you fly from California to Cancun and go live in a hut in the jungle, you may get a more severe case of "turista". You may get the chills and fever for a week and daily relapses for several more weeks. This is because the strains of bacteria are different in different areas. And also because it is simply impractical to not drink water or eat food.

In some more severe cases you might even experience vomiting as well. This creates the perfect crash diet. Talk about losing weight quickly… vomiting and having diarrhea at the same time is probably the fastest way known to lose weight. But certainly not fun…

There is no cure or treatment that can make "the runs" go away. If you have to travel, there are some pills available in pharmacies you can take that will stop or lessen the diarrhea. However doctors say that by taking these pills you simply prolong the diarrhea. But then again traveling with a bad case of diarrhea is problematic.

This is the price we pay for going from one environment to another, especially when those environments are very different.

If you get "turista", drink lots of liquids to stay hydrated as you will be losing lots of water. Rest, put a cold rag on your hot forehead, and sleep if you can.

The good news is that in most of Mexico the "turista" is relatively mild. When I got amoebic dysentery in Africa I lost 25 pounds which is a lot when you only weigh 150 pounds.

Understand it, don't panic, take a few precautions, rest and you will be fine. No pun intended but literally, this too shall pass.

39. Personal Hygiene

These days, personal hygiene products are available everywhere in Mexico. Most Mexicans are very clean. Some of my Maya Indian friends are actually much cleaner than I am. So if you are short a bar of soap, you can most likely borrow one from anyone around you.

Female hygiene products are available in larger supermarkets. If you plan on traveling to the jungle or back country, take a supply with you. For us men, a bar of soap is sufficient.

Certainly in the resort areas or in hotels you will have access to showers. Sometimes the cheaper hotels do not have showers but they will have sinks. As a teenager I took many sponge baths in sinks and they work just fine.

The bigger concern is if you travel or live in the tropics or subtropics during the hot, rainy season which is usually the summer.

Increased heat and humidity causes us to sweat especially if you are from the colder climates and don't have native indigenous skin. I am always amazed at how little my Maya friends sweat when I am dripping wet and on the verge of dehydration.

The heat, humidity and sweat can cause skin to break out or form rashes. This is not a disaster but some types of rashes and athlete's foot can be troublesome to get rid of. Better to prevent them from occurring in the first place.

Take a lesson from the Maya, in general a very clean people. Every night without fail every Maya takes a bath or shower. This not only cools them down in the heat and helps them sleep but makes athlete's foot and skin rashes uncommon.

They also use clean towels and put on clean clothes.

OK. So washing clothes and towels on a daily basis is a pain but so is "jock itch" and skin breaking out. Besides, you certainly don't want to be known as a smelly tourist either.

And speaking of appearances, in California it costs me $18 U.S. to get a haircut. In Mexico, I pay from $2.50-3.50 U.S. for one and the quality is just as good. As I only need one every five or six months, I'm looking at five or six dollars a year for haircuts. Too bad I don't have more hair.

At the risk of sounding like your mother, you should also wash your hands regularly; before each meal, after going to the bathroom and after handling anything "dirty". You will see many Mexicans that are almost "obsessed" with hand washing and for good reason. Clean hands keep germs and disease from spreading and help keep one healthy.

And speaking of bathrooms, you will notice that virtually all Mexican toilets have waste baskets next to them for used toilet paper. If you are a bit on the finicky side and think waste baskets with used toilet paper is gross, just consider how much grosser is a stopped up toilet. Yuck! It is what it is... right?

By staying clean you also stay healthy. Be smart.

40. Staying Healthy, Rested and Active

As the saying goes, if you don't have your health, you don't have anything. Staying healthy should be one of your top priorities with constant consideration on your part.

Of course you should eat well, not too much and watch what you eat. Actually this is not too hard to do as the food in Mexico is generally inexpensive and of very good quality. We eat two meals a day with plenty of fruits and vegetables. Some days we may eat mainly tamales, enchiladas and carnitas but make up for it the next day by eating nopales, berdolagas, jacubes and mesis or papalos.

Don't forget the fruit. But also don't forget to not eat too much fruit at once.

It seems the whole modern world is filled with angst, stress and is sleep deprived. One of the advantages of being retired is that you can get enough sleep so that you aren't always walking around bleary eyed. If we go to bed late or stay up working through the night, we sleep late.

On most days I manage to take an hour or two siesta in the afternoon. If I drink a little too much one evening at a fiesta, I will sleep later the next day to compensate. Sometimes when we travel we get little sleep so we make sure we get plenty of sleep both before and after we go.

Of course you can't just lie around eating and sleeping; you need to get some exercise as well. I don't jog or go the gym but I will rake leaves, pick fruit, wash clothes, wash dishes and walk to the store. I don't seem to have physical ailments or weakened muscles. Sometimes in a city such as Jalapa we might walk around all day and even overdo it, but the next day we sleep late and go for a ride in the car.

But good health is also mental as well. You have to keep your mind both active and at a low stress level; if you don't that blood pressure will creep up and your body will begin to tell you something is not quite right.

Review your finances regularly, take care of your personal business and then forget about it. If you must worry, worry about the things you can control and not about the things out of your control.

Take time to cook, wash clothes, send out letters and email, etc. but also time to play, read, relax and converse with friends. One good strategy is to do some chores everyday but also keep open large chunks of free time to do what you want or whatever you feel like doing on the spur of the moment. That way you take care of your business yet stay relaxed at the same time.

So I plan out an hour or two of my day but unless I'm working will reserve chunks of time for other things. If we travel or take a day trip, we double up on the must do chores so we will be able to enjoy the trip without thinking about all the things we really should or need to be doing.

Some people are regimented and others aren't. You should make out your schedule according to your needs and what you like to do.

However, you will want to have that occasional day when you have no plan at all so you can take a walk, take a bus ride or drive to the next town and simply explore. That keeps you healthy, fresh, and all the little gray cells happily firing away.

With a bit of forethought you can not only lower your stress level to keep that blood pressure down but also raise those endorphins a bit so you will feel good.

And if you keep it up, you might even find yourself starting to feel quite happy!

41. Snakes, Scorpions, Ticks, Chiggers, Fleas and Rats

For my peso the countryside is the better part of Mexican life. But along with the good comes the not so good and the sometimes downright ugly.

Snakes can be a problem. Most of the snakes you see in the wild will be harmless; green snakes, garter snakes and maybe an occasional lancer or boa. These snakes eat rats and mice and some even eat other snakes including poisonous ones.

But some snakes, such as coral snakes and the vipers, can be dangerous.

Snake bites occur when snakes are cornered or most commonly when stepped on. Even bigger snakes such as boas, flee when they sense a human coming their way. But when stepped on they will bite in self-defense, it is in their nature. So rule number one is watch where you step.

Some snakes also love to hang out in trees so rule number two is don't grab low hanging branches or vines.

Most snake bites occur not in the wild but on the edges of cities and towns where humans push them out from their habitat. In heavy rains or flooding snakes also seek higher ground including kitchens and bedrooms.

We had a green snake crawl into our stove and we just could not get the critter out. Finally we lit the stove and shortly thereafter he came crawling out and the dog ran him out into the back yard.

If you go into the very deep jungle where there are no roads or villages, you might consider taking a generic anti-venom kit. If you are bitten, identify the snake or kill it if possible and head to the nearest hospital. Hospitals and clinics carry anti-venom for most local snakes.

Scorpions come in very small and somewhat larger varieties. The venom of the sting can be harmless to dangerous, depending on the type of scorpion and the region you are in. Durango and Chiapas are known for having especially "bad" varieties of scorpions.

If bitten, go to the nearest hospital or clinic for a shot of anti-venom that should do the trick. Some of more deadly kinds can cause the tongue to swell and difficulty breathing. One night a Gulf Coast variety scorpion crawled into my T-shirt as I slept stinging me three times before I could get him. The stings were like bee stings and the effect lasted about an hour.

Ticks come in large and small varieties and are a curse on humanity as well as cattle. Their season is late spring and early summer and they thrive wherever there are cattle. Infected cattle can have hundreds of ticks if not treated.

A particularly bad type of tick is the "pinolillo" that can be found in almost any cow pasture. They are very small and often not seen until the bite causes itching and swelling.

Though not dangerous, ticks and pinolillos can cause a great deal of swelling and itching and if you scratch, especially while asleep, the bites can become infected. Remove the ticks with tweezers or your fingernails being careful to pull out the heads as well. Put Vicks Vaporub directly on bites to reduce itching.

In certain jungle and forested areas chiggers or "coloraditos" can cause great harm. You can't see them and they crawl into your clothing and underwear and bite. Like pinolillos, the bites can swell to great size with accompanying itching.

Whenever I come back from the jungle bush, I immediately remove all clothing and rub my legs with alcohol. Then take a shower or bath scrubbing my whole body. Then dry and do another alcohol rubdown. This process doesn't eliminate them but does a good job of reducing their numbers. Don't forget to take your "infested" clothing outside!

Fleas can be found wherever animals are found especially dogs and cats. Be sure to treat your pets regularly for fleas. Fleas lay eggs that can hatch weeks later and make you and your pet miserable.

For some reason fleas love the dust and dirt. I once stepped on a "nest" and was bitten seven times on the bottom of my foot. For several weeks I was miserable and only found relief with liberal applications of Vicks.

Rats are found wherever humans are found and especially human garbage. They carry diseases and can ruin food supplies. When we moved into a hut in the jungle, it was infested with rats that came out of the bush at night to get an easy meal. We used a number of traps and would hear them go off all night. Finally we got a cat that took care of the problem.

Rats also thrive in the cities going from house to house and traveling through sewer pipes. Use traps or sticky paper to catch them. Rat poison is also commonly sold but is dangerous for pets and babies and I would avoid using it. One consideration: a dead rat will generate an awful odor for up to several weeks so use your common sense. You may not want to set traps if you plan to be away for a week or two.

The above critters can make your life miserable. They can be a threat but also a challenge. A little prevention and common sense won't eliminate them but will reduce their impact. The effort is well worth it.

42. Making Friends

What exactly is a friend is a matter open for discussion and there are various shades of opinions. Some say friends are simple acquaintances and others say friends are the most trusted allies of any human, with the possible exception of family. Some say friends are even more important than family as you can pick your friends.

A friend is one that helps, provides company, provides support and does not exploit.

As a retiree you largely avoid the "exploitation" angle because you will not be entering into a business arrangement or making agreements that require compromises or major commitments.

However you define friends, friends for most people are important; man (and woman) is a social animal.

You may find "giving up" or moving away from your dear friends and family an impossible thing for you to do. If so, stay where you are. But you should remember that just because you move away does not mean you cannot return for a visit. And through the internet you can "visit" whenever you like.

Of course you can always make new friends, at least most people can. You can make new friends if you want to. You have to be open to making friends; if you crawl into your metaphorical cave you cannot expect to make many friends. Friendly people tend to make friends.

I have made and still have many friends in different areas of Mexico. Some I have known for decades and others for a much shorter time.

With good friends I usually get to know them slowly and over a period of time the confidence grows. Some I would trust with my life; others much less so. Trust is built up over a period of time and if one breaks that trust than of course confidence is broken as well.

Unless you know someone well you should not place great trust in them. There will be those that will attempt to gain your confidence thinking they can get something from you. This is the same anywhere you go and realizing this is just common sense.

On the other hand there will be those that will want to become your friend simply because they enjoy your company.

The above is neither all good nor all bad, it simply is.

Understanding this will assist you in making friends and in keeping friends.

The Maya have an interesting way of developing friendships. As they begin to know someone, they give them little "tests" that are simple indications of character and personality. If the person fails these simple tests, they fail the trust and friendship test as well. And the Maya are pretty tough on this; once a "test" is failed, trust and confidence can never be regained; they feel that characteristics revealed in these tests are more than just simple indications. These tests reveal inner truths.

Making friends can be good for the soul and mind. Having friends clearly improves our quality of life and makes our experiences more enjoyable and life a bit more meaningful.

As you will find the Mexican people and culture place great value on friendship and it is something that is taken seriously by most Mexicans. As you make friends you will find that some become good friends and others simply acquaintances.

Such is life. When it comes to making friends, trust your intellect as well as your intuition.

43. Humor, Tragedy, Nicknames and Adaptation

It has been said that Mexicans laugh more and cry more than other peoples. This may or may not be true or perhaps was truer in the past. But generalizations tend to stereotypes which can often be wrong or at least partially wrong, although sometimes they can also be partially right.

To say that Mexicans suffer more than other peoples may be such a generalization.

However it is apparent that Mexicans use humor to poke fun at tragedy such as death, and in the process confront tragedy perhaps more realistically than other cultures, such as the American culture to the north.

In general, a Mexican uses humor and sarcasm to make fun of death and then when death occurs, cry and grieve profusely and then move on. It may seem antiquated and not very chic but modern psychology tells us that this may in fact be a better way to deal with grief. When prolonged grief festers in the soul it can cause anxiety and depression; this we know to be a fact.

So who's to say?

When it comes to humor, the Mexicans definitely have their own cultural form of humor. For instance, it would be considered very bad manners and ill taste to call someone that is obese "fatty" yet this is what many Mexicans do though the use of "apodos" or nicknames.

While to outsiders this may seem malicious or even cruel, rightly or wrongly Mexicans accept this as part of their culture. In fact, many folks are not known by their proper names such as Juan or Maria but by their nicknames.

I know a guy who is tall, thin and slightly stooped over. No one knows him by his real name Eduardo and if you mention Eduardo no one will know who you are talking about. But if you mention his nickname "Vulture" then everyone will know who you are talking about.

For instance, many people call me Gringo or Guero or Whitey. While both terms may have slightly negative connotations, it's how I am known. I am very fair skinned and an American. Besides, Mexicans have trouble pronouncing my name and are constantly looking for an exact name translation, of which there are none.

Some foreigners and outsiders have trouble with this. You may not agree with the propriety but if you are going to adapt and live in the Mexican culture you have to accept it on some level. You can't just go around chastising and criticizing someone who calls someone else by a nickname. They will perceive you as being arrogant, pretentious and even perhaps nationalistic. Your mission is to "fit in" and acculturate, not critique and project a superior image.

Sometimes it is often a matter of context and shade of meaning. I was initially offended when someone called me "muchacho" or boy when I was 20 years old. But later I came to understand this term was used for men up to 50 years of age and was no longer offended.

Grin and bear it initially and develop an understanding as you get deeper into the culture.

Previously I have mentioned the liberal use of profanity in certain regions of Mexico and perhaps now is a good spot to mention off color humor or "Picardia" as well. Just as with profanity, many Mexicans do not tell off color jokes or make double meaning (doble entendre) insinuations. But many do.

Once again, you may not agree with bawdy comments that may in fact border on the edge of being outright sexist. Of course that is your prerogative I am certainly not suggesting you take a moral position here; that choice is up to you.

However I would strongly suggest that at least initially you keep your opinion to yourself. There will be many that would say "that is not correct -- if something is wrong you should come right out and say it." There is a great deal of validity to this argument as well but you should think about the consequences of making criticisms where they are not welcomed, especially when you are trying to "fit in."

Of course there is much humor that is not off color and much of this humor is well known throughout the Latino/Hispanic world.

But awareness is the first step to understanding and if you plan to retire, live and travel in a different culture you should make some attempt to understand it. At least that is my firm belief and that belief has helped me greatly over the years.

So perhaps the Mexicans laugh so much because they feel that by laughing more they cry less. That could very well be the case. So be it.

Such is life. Live with it.

44. Dating, Falling in Love, Marriage and Sex

Ah love, where would we be without it?

Firstly I would never present myself as an expert or even knowledgeable on the topic. But as a teenager I did fall in love with a senorita, got married and have remained married over 40 years. Happily married, I might add as she would remind me.

So my perspective is monogamous heterosexual male so any comments that I make come from that viewpoint.

The standards and procedures for dating are similar to those of other cultures and are a matter of common sense.

Rule number one, and to avoid nasty complications, is to make certain someone you date is not married nor has a significant other. This rule is probably universal, no?

Let's say you date someone you like, maybe desire and feel there may be a possibility of developing a deeper relationship. One warning is that by asking someone out you do infer that you like them, and you should be wary of simply going out with someone to go out as that may not be construed by your date in that way.

Gone are the days when you had to ask the father and/or or mother for permission to ask a woman out on a date. But fathers and mothers are still around, so too are sons, brothers, uncles and cousins that will not take kindly to your "toying around" with their mothers, daughters, sisters and nieces.

Falling in love is another matter and can be very serious business. It happens, as in my case, but you should be very wary. Some men and women are looking to marry only to get legal status in the U.S. or eventually extort money from you. It could be love or it could be love of money.

"True love" can lead to marriage although Mexicans in general now consider marriage primarily when children or a family is anticipated. Many Mexicans live together and have intimate relations as well as families without getting married.

As a male, you can get in serious trouble if a female accuses you of taking inappropriate or non-consensual behaviors toward her. So a general rule is to avoid giving the wrong impression and mind your p's and q's.

If you are interested in a "nice" man or woman and want to pursue a potential relationship, get to know them well first. You can also ask their friends or neighbors about them to see if they are "available".

Be also very wary of anyone who might be under the age of consent, which is 18. Mexican law on pedophilia is harsh and enforceable. Avoid it.

There is of course the ever-present sex for money or sex for hire. Again, exercise common sense. I won't moralize, but you should use your good judgment.

Prostitution is technically illegal although permitted. Brothels are located usually on the outskirts of smaller towns or in "red light districts" in urban areas. Usually brothels have bars where the women congregate with potential clients. In urban areas prostitutes will also stand on street corners or sometimes outside of truck stops.

Prostitutes are supposed to have monthly check-ups and are issued health cards. Be that as it may, AIDS and other sexually transmitted diseases are common so you should always use a condom.

Paid sex is a two way street and lest I be accused of being too narrow in perspective, women also come for paid sex in Mexico. Older women will hook up with younger men and perhaps live with them for a period of months or even longer, and pay them.

Younger women from the U.S. and Europe will come for a week or two and "hire" an escort for the duration.

If you are gay, then everything is a bit more problematic as gays are discriminated against somewhat sternly, especially in smaller towns. But attitudes toward gays are changing significantly and even though gays are the brunt of many jokes, even the macho males have become less prejudiced.

Finally I would have to add that if you are looking at sex for hire, whether male, female or gay, ask, ask, ask. Hotel employees or taxi drivers are good sources of information as they generally know all that is going on. And don't forget to give them a good tip for their assistance and discretion.

So there you have it. Such is life. Have fun, be good and most importantly be safe!

45. Family and the Extended Family

For Mexicans, the primary social unit is the family. The strongest social bonds have historically been with the family and the extended family. Like many aspects of Mexican society, this may be changing slightly, but for the outsider entering Mexican society, strong family bonds will quickly become apparent.

The nuclear family or family of origin is papa, mama and the children. These are where the bonds are strongest. For instance, in the past, father and mother would work and sacrifice all their lives in the belief their children would take care of them in their elderly years.

The strong family bonds can also be seen with millions of Mexican immigrants in the U.S. Parents will work long hours in menial jobs with no hope for advancement so they can provide opportunity for their children.

As an outsider, these strong bonds sometimes make little sense especially when carried to the extreme. Parents will defend their children even when the children are manipulative or abusive. It is not unusual for parents to find out their children are stealing from them and yet still defend their children's actions.

Strong bonds are also seen in grandparents, aunts, uncles, nieces, nephews and cousins. This presents some interesting sociological and psychological implications as family structure changes with modernization.

The most obvious change is seen in the number of children per family. In 1960 the average Mexican family had six children but by 2010 or 50 years later the average family had about two children.

I will often joke with a young couple with several children that all they need is to have a few more and they will be set. Invariably they will shake their heads and relate how difficult it is to raise children in current day Mexico.

In rural Mexico some changes have been dramatic. It is not unusual to see at least half of the children leaving the area where they were born in search of greater opportunities in urban areas or even in the United States. The children that remain usually have more traditional values while the children that leave adopt the more modern "outsider" ways.

Perhaps the indigenous Maya provide the best example. Those Maya that leave the small towns and villages take the Maya language with them. But their children most often will speak little or no Maya.

We see this too with Mexican immigrants to the U.S. It is very common for grandpa and grandma to speak only Spanish and their grandchildren born in the U.S. to speak only English.

The extended family is also somewhat difficult to understand. Any distant relative, no matter how distant, is either an aunt or uncle or cousin or niece. Sometimes if you try to trace the relations through the blood line, the trail gets vague or even lost. Yet the distant relative is still an uncle, aunt or cousin.

So too are half brothers and sisters. They will often be simply referred to as brothers or sisters making it most confusing for outsiders to determine just who are the biological parents.

Of course in the traditional land of the macho it has been and continues to be common for men to have children by two or more women. Sometimes the fathers divorce and remarry but oftentimes not. Men will sometimes have young children and older children as well, the spread can be as much as 50 years or more.

In the modern age, men that have many children and or children by multiple women are finding that having so many children can be problematic. If the father has a good job, the various mothers can take the father to court for support and the father then has to work day and night to make ends meet. It is not unusual to see a 50 year old male with multiple wives beginning to decline in health as he tries to support them.

There is now even a new legal status called "Concubina" or concubine that gives women and their children rights with their biological father. The third world attitudes are now catching up with first world realities.

It is true that the nuclear family and extended family units are changing but they are still prevalent in Mexican society. As an outsider you will be impressed and at times confused with both this phenomena and the changes that are taking place.

But from an outsider's vantage point, to understand Mexico you have to understand the family unit.

46. Best Behaviors, Courtesies and Getting Along

Since you will be a guest in Mexico, it is in your best interest to be able to adapt, survive and thrive. This is accomplished by folks perceiving you as not only respectable but respectful. Even though this seems like simple common sense it is certainly not uncommon for Americans and other foreigners to act foolish and even arrogant.

Of course Mexicans will perceive you as different; if the color of your skin and physical characteristics don't give this impression, as soon as you speak or are spoken to they will know.

Except in extreme rural areas where few visitors go, Mexicans are used to seeing foreigners. And even if you visit an area with few foreign visitors they will have seen and "experienced" a foreigner presence through TV, radio and the internet. In some areas in a place like Cancun, foreigners will often outnumber the native population.

Your success in retiring, living or traveling in Mexico will be determined by the degree to which you can adapt. By being able to adapt well, you will be able to live well with a minimal amount of problems.

How you wish to be perceived is more a matter of how you present yourself than any preconceptions about how you might or might not be. If you chose to be polite, you will be perceived that way. If you chose to be rude and crude, you will be perceived that way.

This is especially true if you remain in one area for an extended period or come to an area on a regular basis. You will see many of the same people time and time again and they will form an opinion of you based on how you behave and speak. So it only makes sense to help them form a positive image of you.

Perhaps the first rule is to make no enemies. You don't need to make enemies. You come to visit, relax, retire and live; not to confront or offend people. Even though you speak very little Spanish, if you smile and are gracious you will be seen in a positive light. So avoid confrontations and offending anyone, even if you are slightly provoked. It's simply not worth it.

Also of great importance are the "magic words" we used as kids; please and thank you. If you don't speak Spanish, they should be the first two words you learn.

If your waitress asks you if you would like more coffee, reply "por favor". When she brings your coffee, say "gracias". When the gas station attendant hands you your change, reply "gracias". When the supermarket bagger hands you your groceries, reply "gracias". When the bus driver lets you off at your stop, reply "gracias".

Watch what other people say or do to learn proper etiquette. On the Gulf Coast for instance, it is considered good manners to say "provecho" or "buen provecho" when passing other customers eating in a restaurant.

Another example is when you are introduced to someone, you should shake their hand and say "mucho gusto" or "el gusto es mio."

When entering to visit a small group in their home or other setting, it is considered proper etiquette to shake each person's hand to acknowledge their presence and allow them to acknowledge yours. As a foreigner you may be given some leeway in not knowing the local customs, but if you can show respect and courtesy then you will create a positive first impression.

In many areas it is considered respectful to address someone older than you or someone you don't know with "usted" rather than "tu", although my dear Chilango friends from Mexico City are doing their best to do away with this traditional courtesy.

When you greet someone on the street it is always appropriate to say "Buenos dias", "buenas tardes" or "buenas noches" depending on the time of day. In Cancun you can get away with saying "hola" or hello, perhaps due to the great influx of American and European tourists.

If you speak little or no Spanish, you will be spoken to and not understand what is being said. Politely, you should answer "no entiendo" or I don't understand or "hablo muy poco espanol"; I speak very little Spanish. Actually I have found most Mexicans very understanding of your lack of Spanish as they have the same problem with English. Just smile and say you don't understand.

A variation on this theme that you will invariably face are those that tell you they speak good English but when they speak you do not understand what they are saying. This is known as "Mexican English" or Ingles Mexicano. It is the result of learning English, usually in school, without learning the proper accents. Here you need to use a bit of diplomacy as one is trying to show you what they know, or think they know. There is no easy way out here so learn to do your best.

There are other types of courtesy that you will learn as well. If you are a male, you will notice that other males gawk and make comments when seeing a pretty female. While this is freely accepted in male society, Mexican females will view your behavior as brutish and in very poor taste. Of course the complaining females are usually not pretty themselves, but that is beside the point. Your mission is to offend no one!

And so on and so on. You will find you will never completely understand your new culture but you can certainly understand enough to present yourself as both friendly and respectful. And with time you will get better and better.

You have to make the effort by always keeping in mind your goal of adapting, surviving and thriving.

47. What to Do if You are Insulted

You are a stranger in a strange land. You are here by choice. There will be times when for no apparent reason, someone makes fun of you, insults you or calls you a bad name. If you spend enough time in your new adopted country, rightly or wrongly this will happen to you.

As the saying goes, forewarned is forearmed. Right?

It is of great benefit to imagine this scenario in advance, what are the dynamics leading up to this event and how you will react or respond in this disconcerting situation.

First off you should determine did you in fact do something that merited the insult? If you made fun of the Virgin Mary, disparaged the national soccer team or stated that all young Mexicans are criminals, then you deserved the insult. Not only were you stupid, but you clearly demonstrated you lack common courtesy. And common sense.

OK. Obviously you are not a moron and there was no known reason for why the insult was given.

The next question you might ask is "was there anything in your control that led to the insult?" Perhaps something you could have said or done to prevent it?

This is a bit trickier and certainly at times not as straightforward. If you cannot determine what you might have done to prevent it, then you most likely could not have prevented it.

So now you have concluded that you have something that you did not deserve and could not have prevented. If you get to this point in your analysis, then you can probably stop trying to figure it out. Whatever was said was not personal or not rational if it was personal.

If what was said was not rational, then you most likely can infer that the person that said was in fact the village idiot and you have no control over what they say or do. And most likely they have no self-control either.

What you do have control over is how you react. If you react angrily and become defensive, most likely an argument will ensue. This is an argument you cannot win, even if you do win; the person is not acting rationally anyway.

In this situation, you should think "what would the desirable result or outcome?" What do you want to happen? Undoubtedly it would be to diffuse the situation, shrug it off and move on. That makes sense, right? It's in your best interest, right?

So the best reaction is no reaction; the best way to respond is by not responding. Or responding in a manner that diffuses the situation. If you realize this in advance, you can do this with little effort. With practice it will become second nature. Remember you are speaking with the village idiot.

At times no response at all may seem confrontational so the best response is one that deflects the insult and changes the subject. If you are like me, you have to bite your tongue to keep from saying something scathingly sarcastic. A witty retort may give you a moment's gloat but an argument will follow, not the result you want, right?

You may agree or disagree with the above but don't worry I'm not going to insult you. But I would suggest you strongly review what was stated above and think about how you are going to react in a touchy situation, because it will occur.

And how you react will determine how you handle the situation.

And by the way, don't harbor ill feelings and resentment toward the person that insulted you. It's not worth the bitterness and the odds are it wasn't personal anyway.

Besides, realistically, what can you expect from the village idiot?

48. Mexican Food and American Food

Food, glorious food! And especially Mexican food...

The first thing you will notice is difference in Mexican food in Mexico and Mexican food in the United States. As a rule, you will find that Mexican food in Mexico is much better.

We seldom eat Mexican food in the U.S. anymore. The last time we were in Houston we ate out at an "authentic" Mexican food restaurant and the food was pitiful. Once you have eaten real Mexican food you will never be the same.

The reverse is also true. If you are homesick for a good hamburger, you will find that hamburgers are just not the same in Mexico. Even the hamburgers in Burger King and McDonald's are not the same. Same corporation, different hamburgers.

So if you want to eat really good American food you will most likely have to prepare it yourself. Most major supermarkets carry American foodstuffs such as mustard, bacon and cheddar cheese.

But when in Mexico, most of the time you will be eating real Mexican food. If you like Mexican food, you are in the right place.

Immediately you will notice similarities and differences. A burrito in Mexico is not the same as a burrito in the U.S. Nachos, a popular food snack, in the U.S., is not available in most of Mexico.

Of course some of the tourist areas will serve nachos and burritos for those of you that insist on American Mexican food. They will also serve sushi and gyros if there is enough market demand.

You will also find that some food items are just not the same in both countries. A good example is the popular "chile relleno" or stuffed pepper. In the U.S., most chile rellenos are Anaheim peppers, a type of pepper that is usually not spicy hot. American chile rellenos are often stuffed with ricotta cheese or cheddar cheese and baked. Sometimes a non-spicy tomato and onion sauce is poured over the chile before serving.

The Mexican chile relleno is quite different. It is made with large jalapeño peppers that may be very spicy. The jalapeno is most often stuffed with cooked, diced pork meat that is flavored with onions, tomatoes and garlic. The stuffed pepper is then rolled in flour and dipped in egg whites and deep fried. The egg is thoroughly cooked before serving, often sliced down the middle and each half eaten with a corn tortilla.

That's not to say that the American style chile relleno is bad, it's just different and some people actually prefer the Anaheim pepper version. But not me!

So be prepared when you come to Mexico to eat a different style of Mexican food with different ingredients and different methods of preparation.

Sample, find your favorites, and enjoy. But forget the hamburgers…

49. Eating Out and Take Outs

Mexicans love to eat out and there are plenty of places to satisfy their hunger!

Prepared Mexican food is available in even the smallest of villages and the variety of places to eat in an urban areas such as Mexico City can be overwhelming.

Restaurants range from the pricey five star gourmet restaurant with international cuisine to the cheap daily "comida corrida" in small, simple "fondita" restaurants. And everything in between.

Of course as anywhere some restaurants are better than others. You can ask the locals where the best place to eat on your budget is. Ask, ask, ask. You can also see which places have customers or are even crowded and infer that the quality and pricing present food value. Customers return when they are satisfied.

When traveling you can also see where the big rig truck drivers stop to eat as they are constantly on the road and know the best places.

There are also numerous "puestos" or small food stands. Sometimes they may have a place to sit down but often not. Mexicans love a good snack on the run and you will be surprised at how many of these stands, usually on rolling carts, you will find with locals grabbing some tacos or a "torta" sandwich before going on their way.

You will also hear many warnings to not eat food at these stands as it may be unsanitary or make you sick. Use your judgment. If it looks unsanitary, pass it up.

You might consider another point. If a restaurant or stand has many customers, it is probably okay. If people get sick eating at any establishment that establishment will not remain in business very long. Bad food is bad business.

And of course you can also get sick eating at a fancy restaurant.

Most restaurants and stands also offer take-out food. The food is served in Styrofoam containers or plates, wrapped in aluminum foil and put in a bag so it can be easily carried. Take-out food is usually not tipped, avoids sit down service, is often taken home and can be shared as desired.

Even soups and hot liquid drinks are available for take-out.

Several other points. If you see an American chain restaurant and crave a good pizza, you most likely will be disappointed. The ingredients and even the methods of preparation will be different. That's not to say that it will be bad, but it most likely won't be like back home so lower your expectations.

In certain times of the year, usually summer, and in certain regions, such as the tropics, food can be quite problematic. In the tropics where I live, it is not unheard of to hear of temperatures at 100 degrees Fahrenheit with 100% humidity. When the temperature and humidity hit this level, bacteria literally go wild and proliferate at incredibly fast rates.

Meats and other foods can spoil when only exposed to air for several minutes so under these conditions you will want to take special precautions. Even if a stand or restaurant is sanitary, food may spoil quickly if not constantly refrigerated before consumption. A bad case of salmonella can not only spoil your trip but create ongoing major health problems as well. Be alert and be wary.

But most of the time you will not have to worry although you may have to stand in line.

And of course if you find a good place, you can become a regular.

So if you are hungry and it's World Cup or Super Bowl kick off time, you might consider a tasty take out to watch the game.

But when all is said and done, there are few things in life as delightful as really good Mexican food.

50. Cooking and Refrigeration

Of course you don't have to eat out every meal, though some of the single men I have known do just that.

You can cook all of your food or just part of it, mixing cooking with going out.

Sometimes you just get tired of eating out or tired of food that is not prepared the way you like it. If so, cooking is a superb option. We eat out some, maybe several times a week, and the rest of the time we cook. Actually my dear wife cooks and I am the helper but you get the point.

When we travel we usually eat out every meal.

If you cook you will need a heat source. In Mexico, there are three primary sources of heating and cooking food; wood, gas stove and microwave.

Wood is impractical unless you have a ranch and a ready supply of wood. As the forests in Mexico disappear, firewood has become less readily available and more expensive. On occasion you can use charcoal, which is available in most towns of any size. We especially like grilled chicken cooked over charcoal.

The microwave is the easiest as you can reheat food and even cook many foods. Unless you go out for every meal by choice, you need to get a microwave. Microwaves are available at many hardware stores and supermarkets. The prices are slightly higher than in the U.S. and the quality may be slightly less but a microwave is essential. Shop around to find the best value.

If you cook on a regular basis your best bet is a gas stove. Electric stoves are rare because electric rates are high.

You can buy gas stoves at most supermarkets or box stores such as Wal-Mart. Prices range from 4,000-8000 pesos or $300-600 dollars. Of course the more you spend the better quality you get. You can also buy gas burners for much less but burners are limiting and most Mexicans use a stove.

If you bake you will need a stove. Strangely, most Mexicans seldom bake and stove ovens are used to store pots and pans.

With the stove you need to get a propane cylinder which holds up to forty liters of liquid propane. The cost to fill a cylinder is about 400 pesos or a bit over $30 U.S. We cook regularly and find a cylinder will last 3-4 months cooking several meals a day. Propane trucks make regular visits to most neighborhoods and small towns. Service is regular but at times, especially in bad weather, service can be spotty.

Many Mexicans prefer to have two cylinders with a switch valve; when one cylinder runs out they switch cylinders and get the empty one filled. That way they don't run out of gas. Cylinders are always kept outside the kitchen with copper tubing connecting them to the stove inside.

You will also have to purchase tubing and valves and it is also a good idea to have a 7/8 inch wrench in case you have to change the cylinder yourself. In rural areas you can take the cylinder by truck or car and have it filled at the propane supply station usually located on the outskirts of town.

A 40 liter cylinder costs about 1200 pesos or about $100 U.S.

If you remain in Mexico on a regular basis you should consider purchasing a refrigerator. Refrigerators are slightly more expensive than stoves and run about 5000-9000 pesos or $400-720 U.S. depending on size and features. Newer refrigerators tend to be efficient and do not use large quantities of electricity, which can be expensive in urban areas.

In hot weather make sure you adjust the temperature to keep items cool.

You can pay for your refrigerator and electricity by freezing food for future use. Don't forget to freeze foods such as beans in single meal portions. Also don't let them stay in the freezer too long so they get a refrigerator taste.

If you have a freezer that requires thawing out, do it regularly to save on your electricity bill.

Since food is a big budget item, in many areas it may be your largest expense, you will find a good fridge is cost effective as well as very handy. If you live in rural areas with little access to stores, a fridge is a necessity.

Of course when you first come to Mexico you can get a feel for your needs and then purchase what you need. But do consider how much you will save by cooking and not eating out all the time. Also consider the convenience.

In summary, if you plan to spend extended time in Mexico, a microwave, stove and refrigerator are very wise investments.

51. Fruits

Fruits are like desserts; they contain sugar but unlike most desserts, fruits are good for you. Or so it seems…as both a fruit and dessert lover I eat more fruits…especially when I'm in Mexico.

Mexico has all the fruits you are used to back in the States. Plus more.

Citrus fruits are plentiful with areas on the Gulf Coast producing vast quantities of oranges, lemons, limes, grapefruit, tangerines and mandarins. Oranges and tangerines bloom in the summer and ripen in late fall around November. From November through March you can see truckload after truckload going to the la Merced or central market in Mexico City.

But like Florida and Texas, citrus growers now pick their fruit green so it will last longer. As a consequence, the oranges are sour and not good for juice unless sugar sweetened. If you have ever tasted ripe oranges from Martinez de la Torre, Veracruz you will never be satisfied with green oranges again.

Apples, pears and strawberries are also grown in Mexico but tend to be small and not very tasty. Don't be surprised if you see Washington apples and Watsonville strawberries at your local Chedraui supermarket.

Bananas come in a number of varieties and can go from 5 pesos a kilo during season to 20 pesos out of season. I usually buy them for roughly 10 pesos a kilo but don't get them when spotted or too ripe as they tend to go bad quickly in the heat and humidity. Except in the jungle where we grow our own.

Pineapples are also cut green but if you live along the Gulf Coast you can get ripened ones from Cabo Rojo or from the Alvarado region. During the season which is May-July big ones can be bought for less than a dollar or 10 pesos.

Mangoes also ripen in the summer and at times go as cheap as a peso apiece or about 8 cents U.S. There are many varieties of mango; my favorite are the orange colored variety called "Manila". There is also a variety known as "petacones" which turn a bright red and can weigh over a kilo.

Avocados ripen in late summer and early fall and if allowed to ripen are delicious. Stores usually sell avocados by the kilo; prices can go as low as 15 pesos per kilo during the season and over 30 pesos a kilo out of season.

Coconuts are problematic as a virus has attacked the trees on both the Gulf and Caribbean coasts, though some isolated trees have managed to remain unaffected. Most of the coconuts consumed in Mexico are from Guerrero state on the Pacific Coast; good pulp but the juice is not as sweet. Fortunately the Caribbean coconuts are making a comeback.

One of my favorite fruits is zapote; a somewhat odd fruit that most Americans have not tasted. Zapotes have a rich, fleshy pulp that, in my opinion, is one of the best fruits in Mexico. Unfortunately zapotes have a small window of time when they are best; too green and they are hard and bitter and too ripe they become mushy and even ferment.

Tamarinds ripen in the spring and are delicious though very sour. They are usually sweetened and made into candies and fruit drinks. Seldom are they used in rice dishes as is common with Thai food.

Also try guavas, guanabanas, ciruelas, colloles and other tropical fruits and see how you like them. You may be pleasantly surprised and find them a great snack instead of candy or pastry.

If you buy more fruit than you eat, you can either dry them or make jellies, jams and preserves. Preserves are made by cooking fruit, such as strawberries, and adding sugar. You can then jar the preserves and put them in your fridge. Remember that if you use no preservatives, refrigerate, freeze or seal with a canning process your preserves will likely begin to spoil within 24 hours unless refrigerated.

Wow. What else can be said? Take advantage of all the great fruits you can buy at non-American prices. You will look forward to your daily fruit ration!

52. Vegetables

When you were a kid, perhaps your mother told you that if you did not eat your veggies a mean old monster would come and eat you up. Strange.

When I caught dengue fever the doctor looked at my blood analysis and said I was so strong that I would have a light case and not a prolonged one. He pointed to one set of numbers and said it was because I eat a lot of vegetables. So fortunately the dengue monster didn't eat me up. Strange.

So if you want to stay healthy as well as eat well you should eat a variety of vegetables. In some respects Mexico has a better variety of fresh vegetables than the U.S. And this in spite of the fact Mexicans in general aren't big vegetable eaters.

We like to eat fresh so we go often to local markets; many Mexicans shop daily and just buy what they plan to fix that day. That's fresh. Often folks that live on the farms will bring their produce into town to the weekly markets, cutting the produce the same day or the day before; no middle man, refrigeration or expiration dates. Again, that's fresh.

Supermarkets also have a good variety and many "American style" vegetables, like iceberg and romaine lettuce, can be found year round. The huge irrigated fields of Sonora and Sinaloa remind one of Arizona or California.

Some Mexican style vegetables, like nopales and habanero chiles, are now found in the U.S. And of course corn, in the form of tortillas, is now as popular in the U.S. as bread.

The best way to learn about vegetables is to go to the supermarkets and open air markets and find out. Ask prices. If you see something and don't know what it is, ask. If you don't know how a certain vegetable is prepared, ask. If you don't trust your memory, take a note pad and write things down. But always ask.

You can always buy a small quantity of something and try it out.

Especially look for those vegetables that are in season and buy those. Tomatoes for instance, may cost as much as 25 pesos a kilo out of season and as low as 4 pesos a kilo in season. That is a multiple of six; the price will vary as much as six times depending on the season.

Now you may think that tomatoes are an essential part of your diet and an essential ingredient in many Mexican dishes. You are right. But at four pesos a kilo you can afford to make up some tomato paste or sauce and freeze it for later. Or buy some cheese and make cheese pizza. Or fix up those delicious tomato enchiladas by the dozen!

So in season you may buy two kilos of tomatoes and out of season you may buy just half a kilo.

You should also expand your repertoire. You may not know what quilites, jacubes or pichocos are but find out. These vegetables are very nutritious, contain no fat and are easy to prepare. You don't have to eat the same things every day. Do as the locals do.

When you go out to eat or are invited over to a friend's for lunch and you see something you aren't familiar with, ask. What is it? How is it best prepared? How much does it cost? When is it in season?

Of course you can go with the tried and true that you ate back home; even in small towns you will find squash, carrots, onions, potatoes, cucumbers, parsley and so on. But be bold, mix the old and the new, expand your horizon!

And don't forget the preparation! For instance, nopales are good boiled but are really much better if cooked in a little oil with onions and garlic. And really superb when grilled over a charcoal fire. So go for it and stay healthy!

And besides, like your mom told you, you don't want to get eaten up by that bad old monster for not eating your veggies…

53. Hot Chiles and Hot Salsas

Perhaps no essence of Mexican cuisine is more representative than the hot chile pepper and the sauces or salsas made from these peppers. In recent years science has extolled the virtues of chile peppers both in terms of vitamins and antioxidants as well as the curative powers of certain peppers.

Perhaps there is still some debate as to the nutritional value of chile peppers but there can be no doubt that millions of Mexicans eat them as a daily staple food. Many of the country's poorest eat more green chile peppers than any other green vegetable so they must have a strong nutritional content.

Chiles are often rated according to how hot or "picoso" they are and the king of all hot chiles is the habanero. Habaneros are small, somewhat indented, orange or green and very hot. On the Yucatan peninsula habaneros are eaten almost exclusively either chopped up with onions and lemon juice or sometimes just raw with other foods. Watch out! Mucho cuidado!

The next hottest peppers is chile pekin which is small and grows on small plants in the wild or wherever the seeds are thrown. Chile pekin is good to have in your garden as it continually flowers and gives an almost year round supply of the peppers. Whenever you crave some chile you just go out and pick it.

Chile Serrano is long, slender and usually green though sometimes red. It can be very hot and is a favorite when making salsas.

Jalapenos are fatter, usually green and perhaps the best known hot pepper. They are used for making chile rellenos and in salsas. Jalapenos can be smoked to make the popular chipotle peppers.

Chile poblano is wide, somewhat flat and sometimes dried. It is not very hot and is used more as a condiment or flavoring than in salsas.

Chiles can be eaten raw or sliced and put in salads but Mexicans usually cook chiles in some manner before eating them. They can be roasted on a hot "comal" or griddle and turned when they become grayish or blackened. Or they can be boiled in water and later put into a blender to make salsas.

Salsa is usually made with boiled peppers and boiled tomatoes, most often serranos or jalapenos that are boiled and pureed in a blender. Good salsas also have onions that are fried in oil which are also added to the chiles and tomatoes in the blender.

Chiles can also be boiled and then dried to form "chile seco". This chile can be ground up and added to salsa making a red salsa or "salsa roja". Chile seco is also used in mole; a spicy sauce with chocolate and peanuts usually served with chicken or turkey and rice.

Most salsas can also be purchased in a bottle form and added to foods as desired.

Serranos and jalapenos can be pickled and canned or put in jars with vinegar and condiments to make "chiles en vinagre".

For my taste, Mexican food is not Mexican food unless accompanied by some form of chile or salsa. There are folks who just don't like hot food or have gastrointestinal problems which hot chiles exacerbate. Still, Mexican food without hot chiles is still better than no Mexican food.

There are almost an infinite array of ways chiles can be prepared and served with food, either as part of the dish, garnish or seasoning to taste. Most Mexicans like their food with hot chile in some form and a common topic of conversation when eating is how hot or "picoso" the chiles or salsas are. Sometimes it can be the main topic of conversation.

Such is life in Mexico. For Mexicans, hot chiles and salsas truly are the spice of life.

54. Tortillas, “Masa”, Tamales and Enchiladas

If corn is the primary staple food of Mexico then the tortilla clearly is its most common form.

The mature corn is allowed to harden either on the stalk or picked and stored inside away from animals and rodents. The hardened corn is husked and stripped off the cob and the kernels stored in bins or sacks.

The corn is then added to a water and lime solution and allowed to sit for three or four days. The water and lime break down the corn making it pliable and ready for grinding. The corn at this stage is known as “nixtamal.”

In the old days women would grind the corn by hand using a stone “metate” and grinding stone. Today women either buy the corn already ground or take their nixtamal to the tortilleria or tortilla maker and have the corn ground there.

The result is a corn dough known as “masa”.

The masa can then be pressed out by hand or more commonly with a type of metal press. It then is placed on a hot “comal” or griddle and when cooked becomes the ubiquitous tortilla.

Fresh tortillas are the best tasting. They are taken directly from the comal and stacked, sometimes on a plate or often in a cloth or container to keep them hot. When eating from stacked tortillas, it is standard practice to leave the top tortilla on the stack and take the tortilla directly under it. This insures that the tortilla you eat is hot.

The tortillas that are not eaten can be refrigerated or frozen for future use. Frozen tortillas will last for several weeks but refrigerated ones may last only several days or so. They can then be reheated on a comal or microwave and eaten as desired.

There is an art to placing pressed masa on a hot comal and coming up with a cooked tortilla. You don’t need to learn how to do this but you should learn how reheat tortillas on a comal.

Comals are available in most hardware stores and in all local markets. The comal is placed directly over the stove burner.

Most Mexicans no longer make their own nixtamal, masa or cook their own tortillas. They buy their tortillas directly from commercial “tortillerias” that make fresh tortillas on a daily basis.

Most tortillerias also sell masa by the kilo. This masa is used to make a variety of corn based foods, the most common being the tamale. The uncooked masa is folded in banana leaves or corn husks with sauces, meats or vegetables and then steam cooked for an hour or so until done. The tamale is served in the husk or banana leaf, usually with a side sauce for additional flavor.

Enchiladas are folded tortillas with a sauce added inside and on top. The sauce may be red, green, sesame seed, pumpkin seed or mole sauce. Cheese, meat, onions or other ingredients may also be added.

The combinations of ingredients for enchiladas approach the infinite. Enchiladas are one of the most popular foods in Mexico and it is common to hear Mexicans say “quiero enchiladas.” I want enchiladas. Once you develop your taste for them, you will find yourself also saying “quiero enchiladas”.

Of course when you move to Mexico you can explore, sample, learn, observe and ask, ask, ask. If you make friends or live near a family ask if you can watch them prepare tortillas, enchiladas and tamales. And don’t be shy -- try your hand at it too. They may laugh at your awkwardness but how else are you supposed to learn?

Not only will you eat well but you will learn in the process. And most likely make some new friends along the way.

55. Bread, Pastries and Cakes

Perhaps the greatest legacy of the French Conquest and French occupation of Mexico was bread. In the land of the tortilla, Mexicans consume a surprising quantity of bread. In Mexico City for instance, bread is consumed by many residents as a late night meal.

Bakeries or "panaderias" are found in most towns. In very small towns or rural areas, women will bake bread in clay ovens in back of their homes and then sell the bread out of baskets. In Mexico City, huge bakeries will make a variety of rolls and French breads as well as an even greater variety of sweet breads or pastries.

The variety is somewhat overwhelming and the only way to find out what you like best is to try them all. If we go to a new bakery and don't have a particular favorite we will mix and match.

To find the best bakeries or best home baked breads you should ask the locals. You will notice a great deal of variation in quality though not such great variation in price. Often the lowest quality of bread is found in large bakeries and the highest quality in home baked clay ovens.

Bread should be consumed the day it is baked or at least by the day afterward. After several days, bread tends to get hard and turn stale. Preservatives are not added in the smaller bakeries so after several days bread will start to get moldy.

Bread is always better when consumed fresh so only buy what you plan eating immediately. Since bread is usually baked daily, you can go back the next day for more.

In many areas bread is consumed with cold milk or in winter time with hot chocolate. We prefer bread and coffee; children almost always eat bread with milk.

The "bolillo" or roll is very common and sold in virtually all bakeries. It is somewhat small and is usually inexpensive. Large supermarkets will sell "bolillos" for as little as a peso or 8 cents U.S. as a loss leader; you will often see customers carrying out large bags as they leave the supermarket.

There are many types of sweet breads or pastries with the "concha" perhaps the most popular. It is round with a sugar based covering over the top. Some pastries are cream filled and are more expensive.

Most bakeries also bake several varieties of cookies which can be tasty but are often disappointing.

Larger bakeries also cook cakes and sometimes pies. Most pies are not very good and tend to be a bit on the pricey side. Cakes tend to be very sweet, especially the icing. One of the most popular cakes is known as "tres leches" or three milk cake. It is actually very flavorful with a type liquid cream filling. It needs to be refrigerated and only lasts several days as it gets soggy.

Most bakeries will sell cakes and pies by the slice as well as whole cakes and pies. Many of the whole cakes are sold for parties and fiestas; if you are invited to a party and don't know what to take, you might consider taking a cake. There is never enough cake at fiestas and if any is left over the hosts can have it the next day.

Supermarkets also carry sliced white bread and sliced whole wheat bread. One interesting and different commercially packaged bread is "pan tostado" or toasted bread. It is good with butter and honey and is worth a try.

Some bakeries also have tables and chairs so you can eat a pastry and have a coffee or glass of milk. I always like to sit down to have a rest, maybe read the newspaper and of course watch the people come and go.

If you love bread and pastries, you are in luck. Sample to find out what you like best, watch your intake and be sure to exercise and walk off what you eat!

56. Milk, Cheese and Dairy Products

In the "old days" there was only raw milk and Carnation evaporated milk. Things have changed. Unless you live on a farm you now cannot get raw milk or cream. I never really did like raw milk anyway.

In fact, in most areas you will not be able to find fresh milk. What you will find is milk that is in a carton that does not need refrigeration though it does have a shelf life of several months. This milk is pretty good though not as good as fresh milk. It is available as whole milk, 2% or and fat free. It is sold by the liter carton and once it is open needs to be refrigerated.

You can also get a type of cream or "half and half" but again you can expect to be disappointed.

Butter is sold in most major grocery stores and is often more expensive than in the United States. The taste is slightly different but still is better than margarine or vegetable fat. In smaller towns you will find that many people don't know the difference and will try to sell you margarine as butter.

Sour cream is available and generally pretty good. Cottage cheese is also available but disappointing if you are used to the U.S. variety. In recent years more American varieties of cheeses are available in larger grocery stores. But most Mexicans do not buy much American style cheese.

This is because if you live in a milk producing region, you have access to fresh cheese. This fresh cheese is some of the best cheese you will ever taste making you totally forget about Kraft singles. Fresh cheese comes in two basic varieties: queso fresco or fresh cheese and queso de bola also sometimes known as queso de Oaxaca.

Queso fresco comes in round, pressed sizes ranging up to one kilo but usually less. It costs from 30-50 pesos depending on the size. Quality varies greatly so if you find a queso fresco you like you should probably go back to the same source when you want more. Queso fresco should be wrapped in plastic and refrigerated. It is best when used right after purchase but will save up to a week. It can also be frozen.

Queso de bola is known in the U.S. as string cheese though it is slightly different in taste. In comes in long strings and is wrapped up in a ball, hence the name. It is sold by the kilo and can range from 70-90 pesos per kilo. I usually buy a half kilo which lasts us for the week. It is also the cheese you want to use if you are considering making pizza.

Another cheese variety is “requeson” or a type of ricotta cheese. It comes wrapped up in corn husks and should be eaten quickly as it will last only a few days even when refrigerated.

In recent years yoghurt has exploded in popularity and even smaller grocery stores will sell it. You can buy it flavored or unflavored and it is sold by weight. We buy it by the kilo that costs around 25 pesos or $2 U.S. Yoghurt drinks are also popular and generally sold wherever soft drinks are sold.

In the heat dairy products spoil quickly so you need to either consume them or refrigerate them right away.

Generally speaking, dairy products are widely available and of good quality. Besides, a good bowl of corn flakes and cold milk will make you feel a little less homesick.

57. Fish, Shrimp, Crab and Oysters

If you love seafood, you will love the Mexican seafood. My favorite city for seafood is Campeche where the fish, shrimp and crab are fresh, cheap and delicious. We will eat fish three times a day and don't even get our fill if we are only staying for a week.

Fish stew and baked fish are two ways of preparing fish that are not as common as in the U.S. Tacos are also a popular way of eating fish but if you prepare fish tacos make sure you take out all the bones.

Some fish that are sold in the markets are very fresh and flavorful but very bony. If you cook your own fish you should try different fish to find out which you like best. Sometimes the most expensive fish is not the best.

Unfortunately for most of Mexico wild fresh water fish is a thing of the past. Many rivers are now polluted and/or have no fish. Fresh water fish sold in supermarkets is farmed. However in some remote mountainous or jungle areas there are still fresh water fish that are good to eat. Chiapas, Campeche, and Quintana Roo states still have good fresh fish, mainly because the Maya don't like fish very much.

Saltwater fish is also becoming less of a commodity, especially in the Gulf region.

I like my fish fried in light oil but there are many ways to cook fish. If you fry fish yourself, don't forget to open the windows and turn on the fans. The smell of fried fish can last for weeks in curtains and furniture.

Fried fish is also available by the kilo in larger markets. Unfortunately it tends to be greasy, salty and the type of fish not to my liking. But don't take my word for it, try it, you might like it.

Fresh shrimp is available only in season, the rest of the year it is fresh frozen. Of course fresh is best but frozen is good too. Shrimp is available in all sizes but we have found the medium size is the best, even better than the jumbo size. Dried small shrimp is available in most markets and is used in preparing many dishes, especially rice dishes.

If you like shrimp you should try the garlic shrimp or "mojo de ajo". If well prepared you will not find a tastier seafood dish anywhere. It tends to be a bit expensive in restaurants but if you find a restaurant that really does it well you can make it your weekly treat.

Crab is a real bargain, plentiful and relatively cheap compared to prices in the U.S. Some of the crab has too much shell for my liking but if you are patient and don't mind picking away at it you can get your fill. Some restaurants and stalls shell crab and sell it by the bag or kilo. Incredibly some of this prepared crab actually has small bits of shell in it and is eaten that way. It's not for me and I would not recommend buying it!

I used to eat oysters many years back with lemon, hot sauce and beer. No longer. Oysters tend to get nasty organisms that can make you very sick. It's not even a matter of refrigeration or hygiene, it's where the oyster beds are located.

As a consequence, restaurants that serve oysters have signs saying "eat oysters at your own risk". In other words, they are saying they will serve you oysters but not be responsible if those oysters make you sick. Go figure. Stick with shrimp.

If you live along the coast you will find a ready supply of fresh seafood available. You may even get to know some of the fishermen and buy directly from them. A three or four kilo fish can feed up to 10 people.

Fish, great eating but a royal pain to clean…

58. Meat: Chicken, Pork, Beef and "Wild Meat"

Meat is readily available in most towns of any size. There are basically two methods that meat is brought to consumers.

The "old way" is an animal is butchered locally and sold locally. Animals are butchered early in the morning and the meat put up for sale that same day. The meat that is not sold is refrigerated for sale the following day.

The other way is through supermarkets much the same as in the United States. Animals are slaughtered, the carcasses stored in refrigerated lockers and later distributed via refrigerated tractor trailers to supermarkets. The major chain supermarkets then cut the meat, package it and put it out for sale.

We buy at both and have not had problems. Of course you should look at the package date and make sure the meat is fresh, especially chicken. A reputable retailer will not sell spoiled meat or they would quickly lose their customers. Contaminated or spoiled meat has serious health consequences, especially if it has salmonella.

Chicken is sold practically everywhere now and is the most popular meat in most areas. Most chicken is grown on "chicken farms" as in the U.S. Most towns have numerous "puestos" or stands where chicken is sold. Usually you will see the owner shooing off the flies.

In rural areas you can also find free range chickens that are raised on corn with little or no commercial feed. These tend to be tastier but tougher. If you want really fresh chicken you can buy a live one but unless you are familiar with how to kill one and prepare it that is not a good option. It's a lot of work and even nastier than cleaning fish.

Eggs are available in most stores and are sold by the carton or kilo. Recently eggs have gone way up in price and are actually more expensive than in the U.S.

Pork is a bit more expensive than chicken but less expensive than beef. It is also tougher than in the U.S. and requires longer to cook and of course pork should be thoroughly cooked anyway. Bacon is available at larger supermarkets but is more expensive than in the U.S. and lower in quality.

Many small stands that sell pork will also sell "carnitas" or deep friend bits of pork meat and "chicharones" or deep fried pork rinds. If prepared well the carnitas can be delicious when eaten with tortillas and salsa. The chicharones are a bit too fatty for my taste but many Mexicans love them.

Pork sausage or chorizo is also popular but many chorizos are not very good. You have to try the local brands to see which one you like, if any. Chorizo is especially good when cooked with eggs and eaten with fresh tortillas.

Beef is very popular but in general much tougher than beef in the U.S. Sometimes the meat has to be cooked or boiled for a long time before it becomes tender. The cuts are also different with T-bones being much thinner so unfortunately you will have to forego that medium rare one.

One cut that is tender as well as tasty is "cecina" or skirt steak. In many areas it is considered to be the best cut and therefore the most expensive; sometimes as much as $5 U.S. per pound. We might buy a half kilo a week or 1.1 pounds and for the two of us as it makes several meals. On the Gulf Coast, cecina, enchiladas and black beans are a regional standard.

If you live in the mountains, jungle or remote areas you may have a chance to eat wild meat or meat that is "hunted". Wild bird can be very tasty but in general wild meat is greasy, gamey and has a somewhat foul odor. One word of extreme caution: if the meat you eat was killed by a shotgun, which it usually is, be aware it may contain shotgun pellets. These pellets can break a tooth so chew very lightly!

We actually eat less meat when in Mexico than when we are in the U.S., especially red meat. This is a plus. When you buy meat, ask around for who carries the best meat at the best prices. Learn the various cuts and what meals you can prepare with which cuts.

And don't forget to try the cecina. Provecho!

59. Beer, Wine and Spirits

Ah, the spirits that make the soul soar! And sometimes roar…

Beer is the national alcoholic beverage of Mexico. In the late nineteenth and early twentieth centuries German immigrants arrived and brought with them beer making skills from the old country. They founded breweries, some of which prospered and later became some of the largest companies in Mexico.

With the exception of microbreweries, Mexican beer is better than beer produced in the United States. The primary reason is that rice is not used in Mexican beer production. This is a plus for those that like to drink beer but also a minus for those that have a problem with excessive alcohol consumption.

If you park along the Chetumal-Cancun highway you will see a steady stream of double tractor trailers filled with Sol beer heading to the Riviera Maya. The turistas obviously like the Mexican beer as well.

Most of the beer is produced in mountainous areas such as Monterey, Orizaba and Mexico City. The early German brewers knew that a plentiful supply of good water was essential to successful beer production. The most notable exception is Tecate beer which is brewed in Baja California.

Modelo is perhaps the best selling beer in Mexico with Corona, Tecate and Sol also very popular. Superior and Indio are other popular brands. Kloster and Tropical are cheaper beers that are gaining in popularity as well.

Mexican beer is only slightly cheaper in Mexico than in the United States. A six pack of Modelo costs roughly $6 dollars in Texas and $5 dollars in Mexico. Corona and Sol are more expensive in the U.S. than in Mexico though both beers are about the same price as Modelo in Mexico.

Kloster and Tropical Light are cheaper running about $3 U.S. in Mexico. I have not seen them for sale in Texas.

Beer is also sold by the liter or quart and is popularly known as the "caguama". Usually the caguama requires a return bottle and costs about 25 pesos or 2 dollars. Bottled beer by the case is cheaper but often requires returnable bottles. Beer by the case is usually only sold at "depositos" or distributors. If you drink a lot of beer you most likely want to buy it by the case.

Beer is sold in most restaurants and is served at most fiestas and social functions.

Wine produced in Mexico is generally not very good although not very expensive. Many stores like Wal-Mart are now importing moderately priced California wines which may provide the best wine value.

Tequila is the national liquor and also the most widely consumed. If you are ever near Guadalajara you can visit the distilleries in nearby Tequila. Tequila is relatively inexpensive though not really as cheap as you might expect. If you buy the better Tequila or “reposado” you can easily spend $20 or more per bottle. I don’t drink tequila so you will have to do your own research.

Another type of distilled liquor is called aguardiente or cana. This is a cheaper liquor made from sugar cane. In rural areas, you can buy a type of homemade aguardiente that is the equivalent of moonshine. Watch out, it packs quite a wallop.

There are a number of liqueurs that are produced in Mexico, the most well-known being the coffee liqueur Kahlua. One of our favorites is a tasty green, sweet watermelon flavored liqueur called Midori. We like it and usually have a bottle under the sink.

You can also buy imported brandy and Scotch but these tend to be more expensive than in the U.S. You are allowed to bring limited quantities of liquor into Mexico so you may want to bring a bottle of your favorite for those very special occasions.

You will notice in all beer, liquor and wine advertisements and commercials the disclaimer “evita el exceso” or avoid excessive consumption. Mexico has a significant problem with alcoholism and the social consequences are significant, especially among the poor and Indigenous peoples. It is not unusual for a male to spend his entire week’s earnings in the cantina leaving his family to fend for themselves.

You should also know that in many major urban centers checkpoints with breathalyzer tests are now in place so never drink and drive. If you are caught you could go to jail, your car impounded and a hefty fine imposed.

So there you have the good, bad and the ugly of alcohol in Mexico. As they say on the commercials in the U.S.; “drink responsibly”…if there is such a thing.

In México they say “evita el exceso.” Good advice. Salud!

60. Juices and Prepared Fruit Drinks

If you settle in Mexico you may want to add a juicer to your "bring back" list. You can buy electric juicers in major stores in Mexico but the quality is not very good.

Many foreigners take advantage of the plentiful and cheap fruits and vegetables to make their own fruit and vegetable juices. When you buy in season the prices go way down; carrots will sometimes get as low as three or four pesos a kilo and carrot juice is a really fine way to start your day. If you mix water in your juice be sure to use purified water and not tap water.

The problem with most commercially packaged Mexican fruit drinks is they have a high sugar content. Some are so sweet they are almost undrinkable, at least for my taste. You can experiment with Jumex and Del Valle as well as other brands to form your own opinion.

Fruit drinks sold in restaurants, stands or off carts are very popular and they come in a number of variations.

The most common fruit drinks are known simply as "aguas". The most popular are watermelon, cantaloupe, tamarind, and pineapple. You can also find many other fruits that are used. The fruits are chopped up or pureed in a blender and added to water with sugar and blocks of ice to keep them cold. They are sold by the glass and range from 10-15 pesos per serving.

Another popular drink is the "licuado" or blended fruit drink with milk and usually some water added as well. These drinks are slightly more expensive and are popular because they are considered to be "muy rico" or very tasty. Most of the fruits that are used in the "aguas" can also be made into "licuados".

If you go to a "refresqueria" or juice stand you will often have the choice of an "agua" or "licuado". For the traveling tourist these stands not only provide a sit down rest but a refreshing one as well. Usually they are located in parks or well-traveled streets and provide an excellent opportunity to view the local populace. And of course they will view you too!

Another variation of drink is shaved ice or "raspado" which is normally done with flavoring but can also be done with actual fruit. Very often these are sold off moving carts.

Of course you can pick your favorite fruits and flavors and learn to make your own fruit drinks. This option is especially desirable for those of us that do not like really sweet drinks. You can do like the "natives" and mix up a pitcher in the morning and put in your refrigerator for your consumption throughout the day. If you are on a very tight budget or are not especially interested in watching people, this may be your best option.

As with many options or alternatives you may do as we do and decide to do a little of each. You may buy some packaged drinks in the supermarket, go out now and then for a licuado or agua and on occasionally mix up your own pitcher according to your own tastes.

In the U.S. most consumers buy prepared juices or frozen concentrated juice. But you are not in Kansas anymore and this is one instance where you can and should do as the locals do and try some of your very own prepared fruit drinks.

61. Soft Drinks, Tonic Waters and Liquid Diabetes

Per capita, Mexicans drink more soft drinks than any other people in the world. It is not unusual to find Mexicans that drink soft drinks for breakfast, lunch and dinner. It is a common sight to see Mexicans carrying a kilo of tortillas in one hand and a 2.5 liter bottle of Coke in the other.

Mexicans also have one of the highest rates of diabetes in the world; in some areas half of the population has diabetes.

Without a doubt Coca-Cola could be considered the national beverage; Coke could also be known simply as Liquid Diabetes. Many middle aged Mexican diabetics have amputated limbs, failing vision and face a lifespan 10-15 years less than non-diabetics. But still love those Cokes!

Of particular concern is juvenile onset of diabetes with diagnoses coming as young as ten or twelve years of age. By the time the youngster turns 20 they will be injecting insulin.

Part of the reason is soft drinks are tasty and made with clean water. The variety is endless and the market immense. In restaurants most patrons order a soft drink with their meal; those that don't order beer.

Coke for instance is sold in tiny 200 milliliter bottles and 2.5 liter bottles. You can buy it in the can, plastic bottle or returnable glass bottle. And it is sold everywhere.

Many immigrants to the U.S. state Mexican Cokes taste better because they are made with cane sugar and not corn sugar. No matter where it is made the amount of sugar in a bottle of Coke is staggering. That's why Liquid Diabetes tastes so good.

Soft drink consumption is one tradition where it is better to not do as the natives do. It is a habit or addiction that is easily picked up and easy to continue. When everyone is drinking Coke it is hard to just say "no".

Of course there are other soft drinks: Pepsi, 7-Up, Sprite, Squirt, Squeeze, Kas, Orange Crush, Jarritos, Manzanita, Tehuacan, etc. One of the more interesting is Sangria, a strange tasting drink that is supposed to taste like the Spanish wine punch Sangria, though that is a matter of opinion.

On the plus side bottled water has seen a rise in popularity as well as carbonated water without flavorings or sugar, such as Topo Chico and Tehuacan. Through some engineering miracle the manufacturers of these drinks can stuff more carbonated air into the water then should be possible so that when you open one it spews like a bottle of champagne.

The key, you will eventually learn, is to open the cap slowly and when it starts to spew out, screw it back.

One of the interesting things you can do with these tonic waters is use them as seltzer water, mixing them with other soft drinks, juices or alcoholic beverages.

I have to admit I drink soft drinks but not every day. My preference is good Mexican beer. If you enjoy soft drinks then stagger your consumption so you don't gain weight and start to look blimpish. And run the risk of becoming diabetic.

If you are diabetic, learn to just say no. You simply have to. One strategy is to carry a bottle of water with you wherever you go. Then when you are offered a Coke, just say you are a diabetic and pull out your bottled water. No one will be offended because every Mexican has relatives that have lost a leg or gone blind due to diabetes.

Remember our formula for success; adapt, survive and thrive. If diabetes kills you not only will you not thrive but you won't survive very well either.

It's like smoking cigarettes; something that is so preventable ends up costing so many lives and causing so much misery. Not to mention the medical costs, loss of productivity and loss of potential.

OK, OK time to step down off my soapbox…time for a cold beer…

62. Coffee, Tea and "Atole"

Ah, good coffee. One of the finer aspects of life. Nothing hits the spot like a good cup of freshly brewed coffee.

Fortunately for you, you are considering retiring, living and traveling in a coffee producing country. You are in luck!

High quality coffee is grown in the Eastern Sierras around Molango, Coatepec, Cordoba and surrounding areas. The cool, moist middle range altitude is perfect for growing coffee and you can see it growing on the hillsides when you travel through these areas.

Most Mexicans however, drink instant coffee, the favorite brand being Nescafe. Nescafe is also sold in the United States.

The main advantage of instant coffee is that it's quick and easy; just boil or microwave a cup of water, season to taste with Nescafe, and voila, instant coffee! In a pinch when you really want a cup of coffee or in the rainy season when the power goes out, a cup of instant coffee does the trick.

But not for me. I prefer my coffee freshly ground and brewed with my Mr. Coffee or Black and Decker. Nothing fancy mind you, and black, no sugar milk or cream. I do like the café lechero in Vera Cruz but when I make it in the morning, it's just straight black, a little on the strong side.

I keep a coffee maker at all of my home bases. When I bring it out I rinse it and run several carafes of water first to get out the dust and cucaracha dooky. Once it's clean it's good to go for the duration of my stay.

Coffee filters are available at most supermarkets though I usually bring a jumbo package from the States.

I buy my coffee in the local open air markets which usually sell coffee beans from Coatepec or Cordoba. I only buy one or two quarter kilos at a time and usually have the vendors finely hand grind the beans telling them it's for a coffee maker. I keep the ground coffee in the fridge and usually buy once a week to make sure we don't run out.

I use Ciel purified water and brew a full carafe. I like to have three or four cups in the morning and it's always good to have some extra if someone else wants a cup.

If you figure the cost of a carafe of coffee or about 10 cups it comes out to about 5 pesos a carafe or fifty centavos a cup. If you buy coffee at a coffee shop such as Café Andrade in Playa del Carmen it can cost about 20 pesos with refills. A cup of café lechero at Café la Parroquia in Vera Cruz

City will cost 25 pesos and no refills. Do the math.

So brewing at home is most economical and doesn't require going out.

I don't drink much tea but flavored teas are available at supermarkets. You can also try herb teas specific to Mexico, some of which have medicinal uses. I do like lemon grass tea which I drank every morning when I lived on a rancho as a teenager way back when.

There are other hot drinks which are popular in Mexico, especially flavored "atoles." Atoles are hot drinks made with masa, the same corn dough that is used in tortillas and tamales. The masa is mixed with water and flavorings and has to be constantly stirred so it will not burn, too much work for me to do it.

Another popular drink is acachun, which is made with calabasa or squash. If properly made it is a very delicious drink.

And of course there is the famous Mexican hot chocolate, made from chocolate from cacao nuts from Oaxaca State in southern Mexico. Another most delicious drink but way too much work for me.

One final word on brewing coffee. You can bring your coffee brewer from the states or buy one at Wal-Mart or Chedraui supermarkets. I also like to have a small four cup brewer as it is easier to pack, takes up less space and brews very quickly so you can be on your way quickly.

I also like to have an Aladdin thermos to put in what I don't drink for later consumption. If you ever come across the older two quart model get one; they will keep coffee really hot for 12 hours or more. Mine is a most prized possession.

Of course you can always take your sweetheart to a local Starbucks in larger cities but for the price of a couple of lattes I can make great coffee for a month. And then buy my sweetheart something else with my hard earned pesos…

63. Water and Drinking Water

As with many countries, Mexico is facing a long term water crisis. Population growth, increased agricultural irrigation, climate change as well as other factors have made water a primary concern for essentially all of Mexico.

In the northern states an ongoing drought partly due to climate change has devastated many rural areas and made agriculture virtually impossible. As rivers dry up, cattle ranching is decreasing, irrigation has become more expensive and dropping water tables have dried up wells including municipal wells. In extreme cases people are simply leaving their homes and moving to other areas.

Without water life becomes problematic and areas on the drought's edge are feeling the effects as well. When wells run dry, water has to be brought in by tanker which is not only expensive but sometimes simply not feasible. Tanker water is often not potable and has to be boiled for drinking.

Strained by shortages and antiquated equipment, many cities and towns simply cannot provide a constant water supply. In many areas municipal water is available only on certain days and during certain hours. Many Mexicans keep buckets and other containers available to fill when water is available.

Most Mexicans now have a tank called a "Rotoplas" on the top of their roofs that they fill when water is flowing. These tanks vary in size with the standard size containing 1000 liters. When the municipal water flow stops, they use gravity fed water from this tank to meet their water needs.

In smaller towns in rural areas municipal water is pumped to large tanks where it is then gravity fed to local businesses and residences. Most farms and many houses also have wells to either supplement the water supply or as an alternative water supply when the municipal water pumps fail and need repairs. Pump repairs can take months and then everyone in these small towns has to rely on well water or sometimes municipal water provided by tankers.

In most of Mexico tap water is not drinkable or potable. Municipal water may be filtered but not purified, so it may contain bacteria and other substances. When no other water is available, this water may be boiled and then used for drinking but boiling becomes costly and is not entirely reliable.

Municipal water is fine for bathing, cleaning and washing clothes.

During the rainy season or right after a major rainstorm the reservoirs become muddy and tap water becomes discolored.

Most Mexicans drink bottled water supplied in 20 liter or 5 gallon plastic containers. This water is sold in stores or off of passing trucks. However, much of the cheaper bottled water is only filtered and not purified so it may be contaminated.

Coca-Cola now sells purified bottled water in 20 liter containers under the brand "Ciel". Ciel has rapidly gained market share and is sold by trucks and in small and larger stores throughout Mexico. It costs about 25 pesos or $2 U.S. for a 20 liter/ 5 gallon container. Supply at times can be sporadic so we use three containers and replace them as they empty.

Purified water should be used for drinking, washing fruits and vegetables and for cooking. In hot weather we have found our water usage doubles so I always have the empty containers ready to go.

Filtered water is roughly half the cost of purified water or 12-15 pesos per 20 liter container. Many Mexicans use this cheaper water for cooking and coffee and the more expensive purified water just for drinking or making fruit juices.

20 liter water containers are heavy and somewhat bulky so it is advisable to get a tilting stand so you can easily pour water from these containers into a glass or pot. A small rope on the top of the stand secures the container so it does not fall.

Purified drinking water is also sold in plastic bottles in supermarkets and convenience stores at a cost of about 15 pesos or $1.25 U.S. per liter. As you can see this bottled water is much more expensive per liter. Whenever we go out, we fill our water bottles from our 20 liter containers.

If you settle down in one place for an extended period be sure to ask you neighbors or the locals what are your water options. Shop around for convenience and price on purified water and you may want to buy a small grocery cart to haul around your water containers. I can carry a 20 liter container filled with water from the cart to the kitchen but would not attempt to carry it back from the store.

In some areas of Mexico, such as certain mountain areas or remote rural areas with spring fed water supplies, you may be able to drink the tap water. Ask and find out first; don't take any chances, better to spend the money and be safe.

The consequences of drinking contaminated water can range from diarrhea to stomach aches to hepatitis so be wary.

Be sure to drink plenty of liquids especially during hot and humid periods. You may find yourself drinking 4-8 liters of water a day and even more if you are active and sweat. If you go into the back country or jungle be sure to take more water than you think you will need. Be sure to carry extra bottles of water or even a 20 liter container in your car. Running out of drinking water is a royal pain.

Next to air, water is the most important resource we consume. Use your common sense and consume it wisely.

64. Shopping for Food

Shopping for food is a function of where you live. If you live a major city, you will have a great variety of supermarkets, grocery stores and local open air markets to choose from. Many city dwellers go the stores and markets on a daily basis.

If you live in smaller town or in rural area, you will need to plan your shopping with your food consumption needs. In our rural home base, we go to the supermarkets and market once a week. In our city home base, we go to the major open air market once weekly and to the supermarket on an as needed basis.

Larger supermarkets will have most of what you need. They will have all types of meats and fish as well as fruits and vegetables. You can also find those harder to find items such as wasabi or capers that you will not find in the smaller grocery stores.

Depending on the size, smaller grocery stores will carry most of the basic food items such as sugar, flour, bread, some meats, canned goods, etc.

My favorite place to shop is the open air markets. I use several vendors on a weekly basis and have gotten to know them on a personal basis. I buy almost all of the fruits and vegetables we eat as well as some of the meats and fish as well. As the vendors know me, especially those that come from the small ranches and farms, they will advise on which items are fresh and good quality.

I also buy coffee, cheeses, chorizo and sometimes tamales from these vendors. Not only are the food items fresh and generally of high quality, but they are also cheaper.

Depending on where we are, we can eat very well for less than $100.00 U.S. a week. For instance, if we are in Vera Cruz, we will buy pork and certain cuts of beef which are of very high quality. If we are in Campeche, we buy shrimp and fish which can be very fresh, relatively cheap and of very high quality.

So one of the general rules is to buy what is produced locally and what is in season. For instance, mangos are in season May and June and avocadoes in July and August. You will sometimes find prices can be 50% or less in season. This is not to say you shouldn't buy an avocado in December, but you can eat your fill if you buy a bag of avocadoes in August.

You can also purchase organic foods although as in the United States, you will pay more. As is also the case in the U.S., some foods that are labeled organic may in fact not be, so use your judgment.

We always try to "buy direct" or from the farmer, rancher or fisherman when possible. By eliminating the "middle man" or the distribution channels you eliminate some of the cost as well as shelf time. There is also a philosophical issue as well; support for the smaller farmer helps keep the small farm solvent. For us, this is important as we ourselves have been small growers in the past.

If you drive and have your own form of transportation, you can buy from roadside stands or even go the farms and villages where the farmers live. Whenever we go to visit friends or ruins we also end up buying some food items along the way. It's not that we are anti-big store but we feel that all things being equal, we need to show support the small farmer who is battling the big corporations for highly competitive market share.

You can keep a running budget total of what you spend or do like we do and simply set aside a certain amount each week for food expenses.

You can cut food expenses by preparing more foods yourself, eating more fresh and less prepared food and eating out less often. Some weeks you may spend a little more and other weeks a little less but if you track your expenses over several months you will get a good idea of what you will spend on average.

And of course you can always cut back on what you eat. We usually eat just two meals a day except when we travel, when we stop when we get hungry.

Although food will be one of your primary expenses if you retire and live in Mexico, over time you will find shopping for food becomes second nature and relatively inexpensive.

65. General Shopping and Shopping for Clothes and Shoes

In larger urban areas you can find just about anything that is available in the U.S. In general, if it is imported it will be more expensive than in the U.S., especially in fancy urban shopping malls. If it is produced in Mexico, it most likely is cheaper.

As in most countries, Chinese goods have flooded many markets. Even pictures of the Virgin de Guadalupe or Virgin Mary are now made in China. (Is nothing sacred anymore?) Chinese goods are not that cheap and as most Mexicans know, are often of inferior quality. I bought a Chinese made pocket knife but when I tried to open a bottle of beer, the opener blade bent double. Go figure.

In most cities you can find Koppel and Electra stores which carry everything from motor scooters to refrigerators. Almost all major cities have the mega-stores Wal-Mart and Chedraui where you can buy groceries as well.

Prices in these stores tend to be slightly higher than in the U.S. but it really depends on the items. Clothes may be a bit cheaper but computers and cameras can be much more expensive. One good way to learn is to take a slow walk through the entire store when you shop.

The local permanent markets or "mercados" are still operational but have definitely taken a hit from the big box stores. The markets are still interesting and you will find items you will not find at Wal-Mart. These markets also have some services such as shoe or watch repair and usually have a variety of stands that sell food. Life for these vendors is a struggle and most complain that their sales have steadily declined over the past five years.

Any town of any size will also have a local outdoor market that is held on a specific day each week. Many larger towns and small cities will have several markets open on different days.

In rural areas, small towns in the same area will have their markets on different days with many of the same vendors selling at various markets.

These markets are primarily food-based; local fruits and vegetables, meats, dried foods, canned foods as well as prepared food for take-out or for consumption on the premises. Other stands offer hardware items, cloth and clothing, local artisanry, and so forth. Take your time when going through these markets and you will find it to be not only a pleasant way to shop but also a pleasurable experience. And a fun place to take your sweetheart.

All things being equal, we try to support these local merchants who in turn support local farmers, craftspeople, etc. Over time you will get to know these people and they will always add a little something extra or give you a particularly good deal. Each week I buy the bulk of our fruits and vegetables from women that come from the Rancherias to sell their wares. What little profit they make does not go to shareholders.

Sadly many of these merchants make very little margin on what they sell. To get their inventory, many take the bus to Mexico City to buy in bulk. The resell margin on some items such as sugar or beans can be as little as 10%. And it is hard work.

In the past few years some of these markets have been flooded with used clothes and shoes from the U.S. Intermediaries buy these goods by the trailer load and then distribute throughout northern and central Mexico. You can actually find clothes that are cheaper than in Goodwill or the Salvation Army resale stores in the U.S. If you go through the piles, you can find good shirts for a dollar or two and pants from two to three dollars.

Used shoes are more comparable in price to the USA but now and then you can get a great deal on a pair of Doc Martens or Kenneth Coles.

We do buy some clothes at these stalls as we keep sets of clothes and extra shoes at each of our home bases. Of course you really should only buy what you need; no one realistically needs fifty pairs of shoes. If you buy things solely because it makes you feel better then you have a different sort of problem.

Shopping in general can be fun and unless you live in very rural areas, does not have to be done in one day. Find out when the local markets are held and support the vendors when their pricing is competitive.

Take your time, get to know the prices, get to know the vendors and don't buy new unless you have to.

66. Prices, Tipping, Charlatans, Beggars and Panhandlers

As in most capitalist countries, prices in Mexico tend to follow the simple rule of supply and demand. Where goods and services are scarce and in demand, prices tend to be high, finding an eventual price point range that can be surprisingly high. Conversely, when goods and services are plentiful, prices tend downward and can become surprisingly low, almost to the point of leaving little or no margin for the seller.

A good example may be a well cooked meal. On the Quinta Avenida in Playa del Carmen, a tourist resort, a well cooked meal may run from 250-350 pesos or $20-28 U.S. The same meal in Huejutla, Hidalgo, an area with essentially no foreign tourists, may run 80-100 pesos or $6-8.

The difference can be a multiple of four; a very large spread. Of course Huejutla and Playa del Carmen are very different places.

Certainly a multiple of four is an extreme but the point being that prices are not fixed nationwide unless you go to Wal-Mart or Chedraui. The pricing strategy of these big box stores is simply to not carry items that do not sell in sufficient volume rather than raise or lower prices according to local market conditions.

If you are living on a fixed income, you should be constantly looking at prices not only on what you purchase but on items you don't buy as well. That way you will become knowledgeable as to how prices are set.

Never minimize pricing if you are living on a fixed income and budget; the pricing of an area may in fact determine not only how well you live but where you live. Obviously you can live for a lot less in Huejutla than Playa del Carmen, probably for up to 75% less.

It is appropriate to tip for many services in Mexico; waiters and waitresses, parking lot attendants, baggers in grocery stores, kids that wash your windshield, etc. In restaurants Mexicans usually tip 10% when they tip at all; many Mexicans never tip, especially professionals. Those that leave better tips are often skilled workers. Go figure.

At restaurants it is appropriate to at least leave something, even if it is not 10%. You can leave the bagger in the grocery store a few pesos as well as the parking lot attendant. I always carry spare change in my truck's ashtray and a few loose pesos on my pocket. It may not be much, but at least it is something.

There are of course many instances when you will be approached by those asking for money who are trying to play on your sympathies simply to get you to give them money. They may hold out a can with a picture of the Virgin Mary on it and tell you it's for the poor orphans that have no place to go. The odds are very high that these folks are simply pulling your leg.

One of the more common scams is an approach where someone will tell you their relative just died and they need some money to pay the hospital bill so they can retrieve the cadaver and give their loved one a proper Christian burial. They even have paperwork, sometimes laminated, to help make their case. These appeals are obviously fraudulent; as if the laminated paperwork were not a dead giveaway.

However you will find some folks begging that are obviously handicapped or incapacitated in one form or another. Use your judgment as well as your heart. Mexico provides little or no social safety net so begging is the only alternative for some. Again, carrying some loose change in your pocket is a good way to go.

If you observe the way Mexicans handle these approaches, you will notice that by and large they are generous and where true need is shown, they will help those that truly need it. However some Mexicans will tell you never to give any amount of money to anyone who approaches you because your doing so only encourages them to come back later for more. You be the judge.

As found anywhere, there are panhandlers who clearly are looking for some spare change to buy alcohol. This presents an interesting dilemma; if you give them money you will in essence be helping buy that which is destroying them and if you don't give them money you will be depriving them of the only thing that gives them some relief from their sorry state in life.

I don't pretend to have the answers and will not be presumptuous enough to advise you on what you should or should not do.

Except to say that it is probably a good idea to carry a few extra pesos in your pocket just in case. And when you sit down to eat in any restaurant, at least tip something…

67. Weights, Distances, Areas, Volume, Temperatures and Metric Conversions

Mexico uses the metric system so if you come from a country such as the United States you will have to learn to convert from the British system. Or better yet, learn the metric system.

The metric system is actually simpler but the conversions can be a bit of a problem. Fortunately there are certain "tricks" or shortcuts to help you convert.

The gram is the basic unit of weight. "Kilo" means thousand so a thousand grams is a kilogram. One kilogram or kilo is the equivalent of 2.2 pounds so half a kilo or 500 grams is the equivalent of 1.1 pounds. The conversion from kilos to pounds is straightforward: 10 kilos is 22 pounds and a 100 kilos is 220 pounds.

The conversion from grams to ounces is trickier since a pound has 16 ounces. For me it's easier to know that 250 grams is a quarter kilo than try to convert to ounces and pounds.

The meter is the standard unit of measure, though many builders and carpenters also use inches or "pulgadas". A meter is slightly longer than a yard. 1000 meters would be a kilometer. A kilometer is about .6 of a mile so 10 kilometers is about 6 miles and 100 kilometers is 60 miles.

The meter is also divided into hundredths which are known as centimeters and thousandths which are known a millimeters.

100 meters squared or 100 X 100 forms a hectare or about 2.5 acres. A hectare will have 100 X 100 meters or 10,000 square meters. The area of farms and ranches is expressed in hectares while the area of lots in urban areas is expressed in square meters.

The basic unit of volume is the liter or slightly more than a quart. So if you put 4 liters of gas in your car you are putting a little more than a gallon. Liters are also commonly broken down into milliliters. The volume of soft drinks, beer, milk and others liquid food items are usually expressed in milliliters.

Temperature always presents a conversion headache. The basic unit is the Centigrade degree. Freezing is 0 degrees. 40 degrees centigrade is hot or about 104 degrees Fahrenheit. Most temperatures will fall somewhere in between. It is also helpful to know that 100 degrees Centigrade is the boiling point of water or 212 degrees Fahrenheit.

It is probably easier if you get a thermometer that has both Centigrade and Fahrenheit so you can easily look and make the conversions.

At first you will most likely convert from the metric system. As time goes on, with focus and attention you will begin to learn the actual metric measures and not have to convert. The same is true for money conversion; after a while you will begin to think in pesos and not in dollars or euros.

So every time you go to the store or market, read the labels to see what you are buying. If you drive, try to get a sense of distance in kilometers and your gasoline purchases in liters.

It is not that difficult and in time you will adapt to the metric system and find that your life will become much easier.

68. Hotels, Condos, Time Shares and Camping

There is a wide spectrum of hotels in Mexico; both in price and quality.

The very cheapest of hotels may cost around 200 pesos or $16 U.S. but you will most likely find then too "beat". They may have bugs, leaky toilets, funky showers, lumpy beds, etc.

Many Mexicans stay at the more moderately priced hotels which range in the 250-400 peso range or $20-30 U.S. In tourist areas these hotels may run from 500-700 pesos or around $50 U.S.

In larger cities you may find older hotels in the colonial centers that are clean, ideally located and could be classified as "quaint" in the tour guides.

Resort areas are pricier but the advantage is there are many more hotels available. We usually stay at nice hotels off the beach and off the main tourist strip which are usually quieter as well as more economical.

Larger urban areas and resorts now have luxury hotels where you can spend a $100 or more per night. Places like Playa del Carmen or Cabo San Lucas have numerous hotels in the $300 per night range. For $300 we can spend a week at a nice, comfortable more moderately priced hotel.

A good strategy is to try a hotel for a night and if you like it stay again. If not, find another hotel. There can be a great deal of difference in similarly priced hotels. We have favorite hotels on the way to our home bases that are both economical and comfortable.

If you are just going to an area for a week or less you can look on the internet at all-inclusive packages that include air fare, hotel, meals, drinks, tips, etc. Sometimes these can be real bargains especially in the off season.

The off season is generally considered to be the non-holiday summer season. The slow season or "temporada baja" is September and October, known to merchants as Septi-Hambre or Hungry September. Children are back in school and vacations are over. During this period hotel rates are generally lower in resort areas but in other areas there may be no difference. But you may find rooms readily available and you can pick the room you like.

It also never hurts to ask for a discount especially if you are staying for more than one night. What you save might pay for a nice dinner or cab fare to the museum.

In recent years there has been a proliferation of "Auto Hotels" or hotels where one takes their lover or escort on the sly. These hotels have garages next to the rooms and take all the precautions of being very discreet. They rent rooms by the hour and are probably not the type of place you would consider staying. Then again...

Condominiums are another story. They tend to be small, cramped, packed together and expensive. Often you can rent a house for what you rent a condo.

You especially want to be wary of condos in the Infonavit Projects or government sponsored apartment projects. Designed for workers that get government loans, these are very small, cramped and sometimes have no kitchen. You will often find hooks for hammocks in the living rooms where residents string their hammocks at night. You may also find your neighbor on one side is running a welding business out of his living room and the neighbor on the other side is raising pigs in his back yard.

Time shares made some sense when they first came into vogue 25 years ago but since then the concept has degenerated into an outright rip off. The idea is you sign a long term "lease" that allows you to use the hotel suite or condo for two weeks a year. Initially the leases were for 20 years but now they can be as little as 12 years. And the total cost has gone from 10 to 15 thousand dollars to 30 thousand dollars or more. For that amount you can buy a small house.

To add insult to injury, your timeshare contract has in it that the provider can add a variable "maintenance" fee at their discretion. Timeshares in Cancun can have a $1500 U.S. per week maintenance fee tacked to your bill. Go figure.

Camping has become more popular in the past 10 years especially in the winter months in beach areas. You should be aware that some areas have swarms of mosquitoes and unless you bring a camper or good tent you will be eaten alive. Also you want to exercise discretion and camp in safe areas with other campers and request permission. Even if you have to pay a fee it is better to be safe than sorry.

We have camped in certain remote beach areas with the permission of the local owners. It's actually a great way to stay in some remote areas that have no facilities. Just be prepared and use your good judgment.

One final note. Don't forget to carry your mosquito net in your luggage. Even in air conditioned rooms, those pesky mosquitoes can ruin your stay.

69. Renting a Room, Apartment or House

After you have decided where you want to settle down, you will be looking for a more permanent and cost effective living accommodation.

If you are staying in a hotel and you like it, you can ask about weekly or monthly rates. Hotels are everywhere and you may like the area where yours is located. A weekly or monthly rate may run a bit more or about the same as a larger apartment elsewhere but hotel rooms are furnished so you will need little in the way of furniture.

If you find something you can afford or is relatively inexpensive, you can still rent it while you are gone for a month or two to renew your tourist permit.

Another consideration is location. If you rent an apartment in the suburbs but you really want to spend most of your time in the city center, you will have to add the bus or taxi fare as well as travel time to the cost differential. There are many advantages to being right where the action is, especially if you like to drink and bring "amigos/amigas" to your room.

Another advantage of renting a hotel room by the month is that you can pack up and leave anytime you want.

Sometimes a family will rent out a room in their house to students, workers or tourists. This can be a good arrangement if you don't mind sharing a kitchen or bathroom and especially if the family appears to "nice". Since it is a room in their house they may restrict visitors and activities. Living with a family is a great way to learn Spanish.

One factor in your decision should be how long you intend on staying in that area and will you be returning on a regular basis.

Apartments and condos are not that common in non-tourist areas. One advantage is apartments will often not require a lease or contract; one disadvantage is they are usually unfurnished. Investing in furniture such as a bed and refrigerator, can be expensive so once again you will need to have some idea how long you will stay.

The longer you plan on staying the more permanent the arrangements you can make. If you are new to an area and don't know many people, it is probably best to settle into a less permanent situation first and as you become more familiar with the area make longer term decisions.

Houses are more expensive but do offer more room as well as privacy. For these reasons houses are also more in demand and the good ones that are inexpensive go fast. Often the owners will simply put a sign out front and rent to the first person that inquires so it is best to always be on the lookout.

A couple of additional points. Bathrooms in Mexico can be very primitive or "funky" so be sure to check the toilet and shower before you rent. After you rent, be sure to buy a plunger for the toilet; 90% of the time when a toilet is plugged it can be unplugged with a plunger.

Security is also something you should consider. If you are a single woman or if you have valuables such as computer equipment or a big screen TV, you will want to make sure where you rent is very secure. Find out the details before you make an agreement.

Many rooms and apartments have utilities included. Even so, make sure you don't leave the lights on and the water running.

If you do not have a car and are renting in the suburbs, be sure to find out what sources of local transportation are available, the cost and the service hours. Many buses and taxis stop running at night.

Don't be in a rush as it is a pain to change places or residences, even if you rent and have little furniture and belongings.

Since you will most likely will pay in cash, make sure you get a receipt to prove you have paid.

As usual, don't forget the fundamentals: network, network, network and ask, ask, ask.

70. Buying a House or Land

You may get to the point where renting is cumbersome and you begin to think about buying a house or some land or both.

You will see many commercials on TV and in magazines for property and houses for sale. These are primarily in the states of Baja California, Jalisco and Quintana Roo where there are large communities of Americans and other foreigners.

This is a tough one and you should proceed with extreme caution. The process of a foreigner owning land in Mexico can be complex as well as time consuming. In other words, this is not a simple matter and can be a real nightmare.

The first thing you should do is an Internet search and read all you can to become better informed.

The horror stories abound and there are many complications that need to be considered. Most foreigners want to own real estate in desirable areas near the beach, colonial towns and areas near lakes and so on. In other words, in the most desirable areas.

If you buy near the beach, your property can be taken over by imminent domain to build large hotels or complexes which are springing up in desirable beach areas. You may be compensated but not at market value. Another problem are lawsuits that may extend back decades which can prevent one from gaining a clear title.

Additionally, if all the paperwork is not processed properly you can go through the entire purchase without gaining a direct title. So be very wary!

Another problem is the Mexican Social Security system. If you have workers either in construction or domestic help and do not pay the required social security taxes, you can be in court for years with each year's court costs becoming more expensive.

Realtors promote real estate saying you can sell your house in the U.S., buy an equivalent house in Mexico and have enough money left over to live forever. Be wary as this is simply not true as many Californians have found out.

There are also many problems with contested properties in Mexico and laws giving squatters rights and eventually rights to land they take over. If you buy a property that has legal problems you could find yourself in court for years and paying more than the value of the property in legal fees. The same is true if squatters appear on your land; a veritable nightmare.

In short, if you are looking to buy property in Mexico it is advisable first to decide if that is really appropriate for you. On careful consideration you may decide that it is not in your best interest.

If you do decide to buy, make sure you do your homework and "due diligence". Many retirees have fixed assets and fixed incomes and cannot afford to lose what they have. Most likely you cannot afford to lose it either.

The rule of thumb is buyer beware. Better safe than later sorry.

71. Investing in Furniture and Appliances for the "Long Haul"

Imagine a scenario where you have found an area you like, you like the people, you can get back to the U.S. to renew your tourist permit every six months and you have seen that you can afford to live within your means. You are ready to move to the next level, establish your home base and settle in for the long haul.

If you buy a condo, house or parcel of land with a dwelling on it, you will have a place you can live in indefinitely, or perhaps more realistically as long as you want or are able to.

You may have also found a situation where you can rent indefinitely or at least feel secure in the fact you can stay as long as you want; knowing that if necessary you can always find another place to rent.

In short, you have found your niche and are ready to make a more permanent presence.

There are two general categories that will make your life more comfortable, efficient and cost effective: furniture and appliances.

As furniture and appliances are not cheap; you will need to carefully consider your budget as well as your needs. You may find these items, especially furniture, in good used condition. However you should understand Mexicans often use something until it is no longer functional, not until they get tired of it and want something different.

The most important appliances are the refrigerator, stove and microwave. The microwave is the cheapest appliance, the easiest to move and probably the first you will buy. If you drive you can pick up a microwave when you return to the U.S. and bring it back with you. Otherwise you can shop around the major stores and find your best value.

The fridge is very large and more problematic to bring from the U.S.; it is probably a better decision to buy one new. If you are single and eat out often, you can get a very small model. Smaller models come with or without a freezer but you should always get a freezer so at least you will have ice. Smaller models also have the advantage that they are easier to move.

Larger models can go all the way up to full size with half freezer but you are probably better off getting a mid-range model.

If you are single and eat out often you probably don't need a stove; you can get by with a hot plate and microwave.

Stoves come in standard size so you will want to shop around for the make and model that best fits your needs. Don't forget to also shop for a full sized propane gas cylinder or two and connections.

Furniture is not cheap in Mexico. Seldom will you find good used furniture and new furniture is often more expensive in Mexico than the United States.

Your first priority will more than likely be a bed. Mattresses are sold separately from bed frames so once again you will need to shop around. Mattresses are problematic in tropical areas as they can develop mold in the heat and humidity. Used mattresses can contain fleas, mites and other vermin as well.

One option to a traditional bed is a hammock. In the Yucatan peninsula and Chiapas hammocks are common and in poorer areas are more common than beds. Many apartments and hotels have hooks on opposite walls where you can tie your hammock. Before you buy a hammock, you should look at different types. If you are not used to sleeping in a hammock, you most likely will find them uncomfortable at first. Cheap hammocks are even more uncomfortable.

After a bed you most likely will want a table and chairs. These can be quite expensive in furniture stores so your best value may be in the markets or off of trucks that sell on the streets.

Chest of drawers, bureaus, sofas, and so on are nice but not absolutely necessary.

You should make a list of your appliance and furniture priorities and work the list in order. Your list may be microwave, fridge, bed, stove, table and chairs, etc. Of course you will work you list according to your budget.

You should also see if delivery is included in your purchase. Pencil out the total cost of what you buy which includes price, any accessories and delivery.

There is one other option and that is the Household Moving Visa that the Mexican government gives you once in a lifetime. You can look up the details on government websites. The cost is $200 and you are given a permit to move your household items across the border without paying import duties. Be wary. By the time you pay for shipping and freight costs you could exceed the value of your household items. Best to be informed.

Over time you will acquire more appliances and furniture that will make your life easier and more comfortable. Start by living simply and adding as you go along.

Even if you have multiple "home bases" like us you will find that a bit of planning pays off in the long run.

72. Electricity

Electricity is provided in Mexico by the Comision Federal de Electricidad or CFE. It is commonly referred to as simply "la Comision". The CFE is a state run monopoly and the only entity authorized to sell electricity.

Of course you do have the option of going off the grid and running a generator, windmill or solar powered unit. Solar powered electricity is increasingly common in rural areas where power lines have not yet reached. But most likely if you do your research (research, research, research) you will find that alternative forms of electricity are usually more expensive.

The CFE generates almost all of Mexico's electricity through thermo electric power plants which are run on diesel fuel generators. These massive power plants are scattered throughout Mexico and have generated controversy as well as electricity: the primary critique being ecological destruction. Mexico also is beginning to develop solar and wind powered technologies as well but these alternative forms of energy are just beginning to be implemented.

A small percentage of the nation's power is generated by two nuclear reactors at Laguna Verde, Veracruz just north of Vera Cruz city. As oil production decreases there are plans to build more reactors but strong resistance from environmental groups has created a series of obstacles.

As Mexico's oil production decreases and the demand for electricity increases, the country is faced with some serious challenges. An extensive conservation campaign, alternative renewable energy resources and a tiered pricing system are all serious attempts to prevent shortages, but at present it appears that increasing demand is getting harder to meet.

All electrical connections to businesses and residences are metered and bills are sent out on a bimonthly basis. The charges can be confusing.

Rates are lowered in the summer months and raised in the winter months, the rationale being that Mexico is a hot climate country and usage soars during the hottest months. Additionally rates are less in rural areas than urban areas and nearly double for businesses.

To further complicate the pricing system, there are three rates for residential use. The first is the base rate, then comes the intermediate rate and then the excessive rate. The excessive rate can be as much as 10 times the base rate. This appears on your electric bill along with your meter readings and kilowatt usage.

If you just run a refrigerator, several lamps and a TV, you most likely will find your rate falling entirely within the base rate. If you use a fan or run a washer, some of your bill will bump up to the normal rate. If you use many appliances as well as air conditioning, some of your rate will fall into the excessive use category.

Conservation is the key to maintaining a low electricity bill. As a retiree living in a residence you should not be hit with very high electric fees. Businesses protest that their greatest cost of doing business is the electricity.

As you are "setting up shop" in Mexico you will be purchasing light bulbs, appliances, a refrigerator, and likely a TV and stereo as well. With all your purchases you should look for energy consumption as a factor in just what you buy.

Although the electric rates are comparable or even cheaper than many electric companies in the U.S., they are considered high by most Mexicans. Part of the rationale for the "high rates" is the electrification of rural Mexico which has vastly expanded in recent years.

New lines, substations, and transformers have brought electricity to all but the most remote areas of Mexico. Additionally electricity is subsidized in many of the poorest rural areas. As a consequence the lives of many Mexicans have been improved, something you might consider when grumbling about your high electric bill.

Several other points about electricity. During electrical storms you should unplug your appliances, TV, computer, etc. A nearby lightning strike can wreak havoc on your electrical devices; many buildings and residences do not provide grounding for lightning strikes.

Because of frequent power surges it is also a good idea to plug your appliances into a surge protector strip. This is especially true in rural areas where surges can burn up refrigerators and TVs.

The CFE is also notorious for cutting off service for overdue bills. Unlike the municipal water systems, there is little leeway for paying late bills and of course if service is terminated it will cost more to turn it back on. Pay your electric bill on time.

Fortunately you can pay your electric bill at most major supermarkets for a very nominal fee, usually 5 pesos. This will help you avoid standing in long lines at the CFE offices as everyone rushes to pay their bill at the last minute.

Electricity; you can't live without it so it is in your best interest to learn to live efficiently and effectively with it.

73. Cell Phone Usage, the Internet and Social Networks

Like many third world countries, cellular phone usage in Mexico has exploded. Even the poor, especially the young, carry cell phones. As in the U.S., if you watch people walking down the street you will see them checking their cell phones.

It is not unusual to greet a younger person, shake hands and watch as they pull out their cell phone and check for messages. You can wonder why, criticize, judge and so on but the fact is cell phone usage is as it is and it is everywhere.

If you bring your cell phone from the U.S. you can most likely "Mexicanize" or "liberarlo" if it has a chip. The phone has to be "liberated" for use in Mexico and this can be done via the Internet; many young people know how to do this. The process takes only a few minutes; Telcel quoted me 700 pesos to do it but a young friend did it for free.

Then you have to take it to a service provider that installs a new chip, configures the phone and places usage minutes or "saldo" on your phone. When the usage time runs out your phone will not work until you purchase more usage time.

Time or "saldo" can be purchased at major supermarkets, convenience stores such as Oxxo or service provider locations which have popped up everywhere.

There are two main providers, Telcel and Movistar. Ask those that have cell phones about the services provided. Telcel is the largest provider and is linked with Telefonos Mexicanos. Service is much more expensive than Movistar but coverage is wider and in more areas.

Movistar has lowered its rates and now has an affordable service to calls in the U.S. It seems that I have had one problem after another with Telcel. When I bought a phone from Telcel and it did not work, Telcel charged me usage time to call Mexico City to have the problem fixed, even though the phone was theirs. Go figure.

A phone call with Telcel can run 3-5 pesos or more per minute or about 25-35 cents U.S. per minute. With Movistar the charge is about one peso or 8 cents U.S. per minute. The world's richest man owns Telcel.

Most Mexicans access the internet through their cell phones. There is a charge for internet usage but it is less than making a phone call. If you want to have an internet connection in your residence you will have to have a landline phone installed by Telcel and pay for that service as well as the internet service. As in the U.S., friends and neighbors that live close by can access the connection via the modem and the modem code. The service is called Infinitum and provided by Telcel or Telefonos Mexicanos.

Many small towns and even villages also provide public access Wi-Fi, often at the central park. This service is provided so poor students can gain internet access, which is also available at local internet cafes but at an hourly cost.

With improved Internet access has come access to social networks, such as Twitter and Facebook. Mexicans, especially younger Mexicans, spend hour after hour on these networks. Such is the modern age.

One additional comment. If you have a good internet connection, you can video conference through Skype and Facebook with friends and relatives anywhere, especially if they too have a good connection. If the connection is weak or sporadic, you can still communicate by turning off the video and just using the audio.

In summary, cell phones are everywhere, internet connections are everywhere, and social networks are everywhere. The only exceptions would be in very rural areas or very small towns.

Clearly in Mexico, you can now get connected and stay connected.

74. Laundry and Washing Clothes

In the good old days, the only option for washing clothes was doing it by hand. If you did not do it by hand yourself, you had to find someone to do it for you. Usually the charge was per item, for instance 3 pesos per shirt, blouse, pants or skirt. Usually you had to provide the detergent.

If you lived in town and had running water, washing was much easier. If not you had to carry in buckets of water or more likely, head to the local river. There you would probably find a number of women washing their clothes while their children played on the river's edge.

At the river, clothes are washed on rocks. They can be dried on rocks or draped on nearby trees.

In town, clothes washed by hand are normally done in a "batea", which is a combination washboard and sink.

No matter what method you use, it's hard work. If you have ever washed clothes by hand you realize it is not an easy thing to do, at least in my opinion. And time consuming.

Then the laundry has to be hung out to dry. In the rainy season, this can be problematic. During wet weather clothes often have to be hung indoors and sometimes they do not dry quickly enough and turn "sour" giving off a foul odor. The odor is unmistakable and you can easily smell someone that is wearing "soured" clothes. Not good because they have to rewashed.

Ah, the joys of doing laundry.

Fortunately things have changed or at least somewhat. There are still women that wash clothes for a living at the river and if you live in rural area this may be your only option. But the washing machine era has arrived, at least in urban areas.

Of course you can buy your own washing machine. You obviously have to have running water and the hookups as well. You can also get a dryer but you need to consider whether to power the dryer by gas or electricity; remember electricity is expensive and clothes dryers suck up a lot of juice. If you don't have a dryer you need to have a clothesline to dry your wet clothes. And keep your eyes open for a surprise rainstorm.

A new washing machine runs about 6000 pesos or around $500 U.S.

Detergent and fabric softeners are found at even the smallest of neighborhood stores. Of course if you buy detergent in bulk you get a better price. Shop around, especially in the larger supermarkets.

Coin operated laundries are not common though you may find one if you live in a city. Larger hotels do have some form of laundry service and some even have coin operated washers.

Forget ironing, at least from my point of view. I normally wear T-shirts and pants that never need ironing and unless you are going to a wedding or fancy fiesta you don't need to have ironed clothes. It is also a matter of taste; my taste is casual though yours may be different.

Another option in smaller cities are laundry service businesses that wash, dry and fold and perhaps iron your clothes for you. The charge is by the kilo; your dirty clothes are weighed when you bring them in and you are told the price. Your clothes are washed, dried and folded and usually available to be picked up the next day.

Laundry services charge around 15 pesos or $1.25 U.S. per kilo of laundry. The heavier your clothes, the more you pay.

A few other laundry pointers.

Unless you sweat profusely or get dirty, you can normally wear shirts, pants, and dresses for more than one day. You can also have worn clothes that you can wear around the house. We have lots of older clothes and also keep a set of clothes at each of our home bases. When we go to the States we take very few clothes with us and always bring back "new" clothes or new used clothes.

Plan in advance, find your best options and you will seldom find yourself with nothing clean to wear.

Ah the joys of dirty laundry…

75. History

The history of Mexico is divided into two eras; the pre-conquest and post-conquest. Students of Mexican history usually start at the conquest and work forward or backward.

The Spaniards under Hernan Cortez arrived in Mexico in the early 16th Century and an army of three hundred men eventually conquered a land inhabited by an estimated 20-25 million indigenous peoples. These original peoples are generally considered to be descendants of indigenous peoples that migrated from Asia, down the western North American coast and eventually settling on what is today the Gulf Coast on the Gulf of Mexico.

The first signs of settlements go back to 5,000 B.C. with the Olmecs in what is today the State of Tabasco. Although the exact lineage is vague, most indigenous groups are considered to have come from the Olmecs. The best known groups were the Aztecs in the northern plateau in what is today Mexico City and the Maya who settled throughout the Yucatan peninsula.

Cortez is an example of both the paradoxical nature and the difficulty Mexican history presents for the student. Even though most Mexicans carry Spanish blood, there is a great deal of animosity toward Cortez in the manner in which he brutally subdued the indigenous peoples.

For several hundred years in what is generally known as the Colonial period, Mexico was ruled by the Spaniards. The Spaniards viewed Mexico as a colony that was to be exploited by whatever means possible with the riches being funneled back to Spain.

Eventually the French took over from the Spaniards and ruled until the early 19th century when insurgents under Benito Juarez threw out the French and declared Mexico a sovereign nation.

For another century an oligarchy of powerful rulers of Spanish descent continued the plunder and exploitation of the indigenous peoples. In 1910 under the initial leadership of Francisco Madero, a wealthy landowner, the Mexican Revolution began. The Revolution lasted 10 years and over a million Mexicans died.

When I first came to Mexico I would ask those that lived through the Revolution what it was like. The response was muted and one of horror; it reminded me of the response I got in Spain when asking folks about what it was like during the Spanish Civil War.

Madero oddly enough was against giving the native indigenous people their own land. He was later assassinated and two leaders emerged, Emiliano Zapata in the south and Pancho Villa in the north. Zapata was a farmer who was able to unify his people and eventually march triumphantly into Mexico City.

Pancho Villa was a mule skinner and small time bandit that was able to coalesce forces in the north and move into Mexico City to meet Zapata. Both Villa and Zapata were later assassinated.

Eventually a constitution was written but politics remained unstable until President Lazaro Cardenas took control in 1930's. Cardenas carried out a number of reforms, stabilized the land situation in rural areas through the ejido system and nationalized the oil industry.

Cardenas remains Mexico's most revered modern president. In modern times a succession of Presidents have both modernized the country and ransacked its treasury and resources.

And since the Revolution a succession of Presidents have vowed to eliminate poverty but today Mexico still has a majority of its citizens living in poverty. In recent years wealth has become concentrated into fewer hands and the drug cartel wars have dampened economic growth.

Still the Mexican people remain hopeful though realistic that at some point in the not too distant future the ideals of Francisco Madero and Emiliano Zapata and the Revolution will become reality.

And the story continues…

76. Government and Politics

Mexico is a democratic republic with a national constitution. It has three levels of government: federal, state and municipal.

The federal government is responsible for foreign affairs, national policy, education, the army and navy, federal police, most of the taxes, roads, national health care, etc. When you cross into Mexico and go through customs and get your tourist and vehicle permits you are under the auspices of the federal government. The federal government also manages the oil industry or Petroleos Mexicanos (Pemex) and the national electric company Comision Federal de Electricidad (CFE).

Like the U.S., the Mexican federal government has a President, Congress and Supreme Court.

There are 32 states in Mexico with each having a Governor and State Legislature. The State is responsible for the state police, state universities, state law, local civil protection in disasters, etc.

There are over 3200 municipalities in Mexico. Each has an elected mayor or Presidente Municipal. Municipalities are responsible for local municipal police, fire departments, paving local streets, municipal water supplies, sewage, garbage collection, business permits and markets, etc.

There are three main political parties all roughly equivalent in strength. They are the Partido Accion Nacional (PAN), Partido Revolucionario Institucional (PRI) and the Partido Revolucionario Democrático (PRD). The PAN is considered conservative, the PRI centrist or slightly to the left and the PRD leftist or progressive.

There are other smaller political parties but all have support in the low single digits.

Because of the three party system with all parties being more or less equivalent, most legislation requires the cooperation of at least two of the parties. This can be a strength as well as a weakness; there is a strong system of checks and balances on extreme legislation but true reforms in many areas are very difficult to accomplish as at least two of the parties must agree.

As in the U.S., most Mexicans when asked express a pessimistic view of the political process and outcomes. There is a strong sense of resignation and a low level of expectation. This has to do partly with the evolution and nature of Mexican politics as well as the fact that political systems worldwide have become less and less able to effectively deal with the complex problems of the modern world.

Relations with the U.S. are generally good though at times all politicians express public outrage with U.S. policies that appear to be counter to Mexican interests. Be that as it may, the retiree or tourist may hear numerous anti-U.S. sentiments but rarely will an individual be accused of being responsible for the perceived injustices. Mexicans in general may not like the American government but they like Americans.

It is prudent to be circumspect when presenting views highly critical of Mexican politics and government. It is OK when Mexicans severely criticize their own government but is quite another thing when you as an outside guest generate such criticisms. It's like butting in on a family squabble.

When asked my views on internal Mexican politics I usually state that the problem is similar to the problem in the U.S.; it's not so much the government or the system as it is the politicians. I find this a good response as essentially no one can deny that politicians are to blame especially when you openly state the U.S. has the same problem.

As you get to know people more intimately you may feel free to express your opinions more openly but even so you should be aware that politics is like religion or sports and many people take theirs very personally.

I do find it of value to be interested in the internal affairs and ask questions freely when you do not understand something. This is almost always taken in a very positive light and shows your interest and respect for your "adopted home".

If someone severely criticizes the U.S. government you can either agree or state that all governments have weaknesses. Like religion, arguing over politics is an argument you will never win. And even if you do win, you really don't win, right?

So there it is. And once again like religion, you don't always have to agree on politics, but you should always be respectful.

77. Economy

Mexico has a free market capitalistic economy.

The Federal Government has virtually total control over economic policy including monetary controls. The power of the Federal Government is largely concentrated in the office of the President.

Economically Mexico is largely dependent on its neighbor to the north, the U.S., by far the largest importer of Mexican products. In general the northern Mexican states or northern tier of the country is the most affluent and the southern states or the southern tier is the poorest.

It is now estimated that tourism, including several million American retirees, has overtaken oil as the county's largest industry. For the past five years the Riviera Maya, the Cancun - Playa del Carmen- Tulum corridor, has been the fastest growing region in all of Latin America.

However, recent estimates put 55% of the population or 60,000,000 Mexicans living in poverty. Approximately 20-25 million Mexicans live in abject or extreme poverty meaning they have no savings and live from day to day. There is no social safety net to speak of although in recent years, under PAN party Presidents, minimal assistance social programs have been instituted for the very poor and elderly.

Although Mexico is considered to be a third world country it is also considered to be an emerging nation meaning that the economy is on an upward trend. For a small percentage of Mexicans the economy is very, very good.

It is estimated that half of the country's wealth is concentrated among the ten wealthiest Mexican families. Very few nations in the world have the level of wealth distribution disparity as does Mexico.

It is also estimated that up to half of Mexico's working population works for subsistence wages or in the underground economy. The average wage of these workers is about 125-150 pesos a day or a little over $10 U.S. per day.

Officially it is stated that part of the economic disparity and lack of social programs is the inability of the government to both levy and collect taxes. This is a sore point with many Mexicans as the political parties take opposite sides on the major issues.

Perhaps the biggest economic issue is the inability of the economy to create sufficient quality jobs for the youth entering the workforce. As a consequence many university and skilled workers are underemployed doing unskilled jobs. Lack of opportunity is also what drives many younger workers to look for work in the U.S.

As a consequence Mexico faces a severe "brain drain" as it loses many of its most talented and skilled workers to foreign countries such as the United States. Once abroad these skilled workers join many other skilled immigrants who do not return home to Mexico. The loss for Mexico is permanent.

On the macro-economic upside Mexico's balance of payments, growing international trade and internal markets have helped keep Mexico in the emerging nation category.

But both politicians and economists freely admit that rampant poverty and insecurity have combined to keep the lid on economic growth. For the almost 100 years since the Mexican Revolution ended, governments have promised to eradicate poverty with little progress being made.

Perhaps the greatest economic fear is that the U.S. will have a lengthy prolonged recession or depression and drag the Mexican economy down as well.

In the modern world of changing economic fundamentals it is clear that few if any have the answers or even the ability to predict the near term future let alone the longer term future.

The current Presidente has instituted a wide range or political, economic and structural reforms. The effect of these reforms is not clearly understood and it may take years for the effects to be realized.

Subsequently 115,000,000 Mexicans will simply have to wait and see.

78. Taxes and Insurance

For retirees on fixed incomes, taxes and insurance have become real burdens in the United States. As governments at all levels struggle for revenues, taxes have gone up way beyond levels of inflation. If you own a home in Houston worth $150,000 U.S., you might find yourself paying up to $5,000 U.S. in property taxes per year. This is after you have paid for your home and does not include any repairs or maintenance costs. Do the math.

As for insurance, just try buying health insurance in the U.S. if you are over 60. As the saying goes, you best be sitting down when you get a quote.

A big plus in Mexico for retirees is that taxes, insurance fees and insurance requirements tend to be much less than in the United States.

Of course many would argue this is why Mexico is such a poor country with few social programs and substandard infrastructure, such as highways. But all is relative, you get what you pay for and for those looking at living on a fixed income, lowering expenses is the primary method to make ends meet. Again, do the math.

For instance, property taxes may be as little as 5% of what they would be in the United States. Property taxes in rural areas are almost non-existent. As a consequence housing costs are much cheaper.

Income taxes do not apply to foreigners and you only pay taxes on what you might earn in Mexico. And since as a tourist you will not be working or running a business, you will not pay income taxes.

The primary sales tax is called the IVA or value added tax which is a hefty 16%. If you shop at stores such as Wal-Mart, your sales receipt will clearly state which items are subject to the IVA tax. Unfortunately the IVA tax is also added to your electric bill, but since you will of course be conserving wherever you can, you should not pay too much tax.

Health insurance in Mexico is normally available only to Mexican citizens and not to foreigners. Since you most likely will be using private pay services anyway, this should not be a factor in your health care decisions. You can go to the doctor with what you save on health care premiums.

Car insurance is not required in Mexico and if you do not drive a car, insurance is even less an issue.

If you are considering purchasing a house, condo, land, etc. you should inquire about possible taxes that may be applicable.

Many retirees I have spoken with throughout the U.S. have lamented that rising taxes and insurance premiums have undermined their retirement plans. Many have had to sell their homes, continue working, look for part time work, etc.

If you are perplexed at how you will pay increased taxes and insurance fees in your retirement, you might seriously consider retiring to Mexico.

79. Social and Socioeconomic Structure

The elephant in the room is bias, prejudice and at times outright racism. It may not be pleasant but it is an undeniable reality. Such is life.

Outright prejudice comes in two varieties; skin color and physical ethnic attributes and socioeconomic status. Many Mexicans, especially those with European and light features, will vehemently deny there is prejudice in Mexico. They will point to ongoing racial tensions in the U.S. and other countries and proudly state "we have no such problems in Mexico."

You will also hear "we don't have the black/white problems the U.S. has." Of course not. In a country of 115 million there are only an estimated 50,000 Blacks.

The truth is that just because the U.S. and other nations have racial and prejudice problems does not mean Mexico does not have such problems.

Since Cortez conquered the Aztecs, lighter skinned Mexicans of European descent have been "on the top of the heap." Seldom in TV, movies or magazines will you find indigenous faces unless they are portrayed as cooks, gardeners, servants or taxi-drivers.

You will see prejudice wherever you go and might be surprised at how supposedly educated and cultured light skinned Mexicans will speak despairingly and openly to indigenous people. Reality is reality.

My wife and I present a real schizoid problem for prejudice wherever we go. My wife is very indigenous looking; brown skin, black hair, brown eyes, etc. All of my ancestors were of German origin with light skin, green eyes, light brown hair, etc.

Obviously we present a clear mismatch. The first time we went together to Mexico City people assumed she was my maid. Light skinned people like me just don't marry indigenous looking people like her. But such is life. Go figure.

Another type of prejudice is economic. One of the strangest things you will see is a very indigenous looking person, nicely dressed and driving a car, acting arrogant towards someone that looks exactly like them.

Imagine a soccer star that has the education of a third grader, and the mentality as well, will be viewed as high society because he has money and drives a BMW. Go figure.

However all is not negative. Women and gays have made great

strides in the past few decades. Gays are more open now; in the past they had to stay in the closet or move to urban areas where gay life was more tolerated.

Women can now be seen as having made great strides professionally and economically. It is common now to see women owned businesses now where just several decades back they were a rarity.

What is truly ironic is to see the macho males now allowing their wives to support them and their families. There is no shame when asking the wife for cantina money on Saturday night.

You may not approve of prejudice nor like it but you will see it so you may as well "get used to it." It may be counterproductive and not in your best interests to confront and argue; perhaps the best way to be non-prejudicial and not arrogant is simply to show it.

Your mission is to continually learn, grow and expand your perspective so you can adapt and survive. By setting an exemplary example, you have already changed the world.

80. Indigenous Populations

When Cortez landed with his army and "conquered" Mexico in the 16th century, all of the native born population was indigenous. They were descendants from the early migrants that crossed the Bering Strait and migrated until they arrived at what is today Mexico.

Their descendants today live throughout Mexico with populations located regionally though migration is slowly "diluting" some areas of their ethnic purity. Almost all Mexicans today are a mixture of European/Spanish blood and Indigenous blood. Very few Mexicans are "pure"; that is, all European or all Indigenous.

Somewhere along the line in most family trees some "outside" blood got mixed in. For that reason most Mexicans are characterized today as "mestizo" or of mixed blood.

Some of the major Indigenous groups are the Maya of Yucatan and Chiapas, the Totonacs of Veracruz, the Huastecs of Veracruz and Tamaulipas, the Yaqui of Sonora, the Tarahumara of Chihuahua and the Tarascans of Michoacán. There are several dozen major groups left and you can do an internet search to find their locations, languages and cultural attributes.

I have lived in the Huasteca region in Northeast Mexico and the Maya region of the Yucatan. The Maya are much more numerous than other groups and there are many areas in the more remote jungle areas where only Maya is spoken. In La Huasteca, Huasteco is spoken by fewer and fewer people.

In the Yucatan peninsula, there is great concern that the Maya language and culture is also dying out. For instance, the government requires that all children attending public school wear uniforms and speak Spanish. Kids of course can pick up languages very quickly and the Maya children are no exception; those that enter kindergarten and the first grade speaking only Maya are usually fluent in Spanish by the third grade.

Subsequently children with Maya speaking parents may still speak Maya and understand Maya but speak Spanish with their brothers and sisters. As a general rule, once Maya children start speaking Spanish they stop speaking Maya. Such is life.

From the Maya I have known, once they go and work in Cancun for a couple of years they no longer wish to return to their Maya traditions. Even if they return back to their original homes to live, they have acculturated and are changed for life. Literally and figuratively they can no longer return home.

There is much talk about preserving the Maya language and tradition but to be honest I have not heard of a viable way to make that happen.

The Indigenous peoples are Mexico's poorest and economic change and improvement is slow in the making. There is no magic cure. Education is the best method for improving Indigenous people's circumstances, at least the politicians say so. Progress is slow and not very steady either.

For the visitor Indigenous peoples do offer a wide array of culture and tradition that are interesting while they last. You might even try to learn some native language or dialect but be forewarned, it's not easy. Maya for instance, has no formal grammar and cannot be learned like a Romance language.

Still, if you decide to live in an area that is predominantly Indigenous you should absorb as much of the culture as possible. Students fly from all around the world to do just that and you have the advantage of already being there.

Some of my best friends are Indigenous so I can vouch there are some really great people you can get to know. They are warm, friendly and extremely trustworthy. Perhaps they are a little bit wary of outsiders though. At least at first and until they get to know you.

After all, remember what Cortez did with only 300 men…

81. Religion and Spirituality

When the Spaniards conquered Mexico in the early sixteenth century, they brought with them Catholic priests known as Jesuits. The Indigenous peoples were converted by the Jesuits, either voluntarily or involuntarily.

As a consequence Mexico remains a Catholic country today with estimates ranging from 75-90%. These percentages are down from 50 years ago when 95% plus of all Mexicans were Catholics.

The remaining percentages are divided up between the Evangelicals or Pentecostals and the Mormons, with smaller groups such as the Jehovah's Witnesses making up the remainder. What is interesting about many of these groups is they feel that other religions are more a part of the devil than non-believer Skeptics, Atheists and Agnostics. Perhaps the reasoning is they can never convert the Skeptic but the faithful of other religions are always fair game.

Especially noticeable is the rising ill will between the Catholic Church and groups like the Jehovah's Witnesses. It is not unusual to see nasty barbs exchanged between groups. It is common to see signs outside Catholic homes stating "we are Catholics so don't come knocking with your propaganda."

Such is religion…

There is however a more prevalent dynamic at work. If you sit outside any church of any denomination and watch people leave worship services you will primarily see middle aged and elderly women and children. Men attend church for baptisms, weddings and funerals but rarely at other times; not all men of course, but the vast majority.

As in the developed world some churches are trying to retain and convert the younger generations by guitar playing at worship services, having youth groups and events specifically catering to the interest of younger members and so on. To date, these strategies do not appear to be working.

People no longer believe as fervently in organized religion as a philosophy of life but now accept religion as tradition and social networking.

What is noticeable particularly among the young are more generalized spiritual events and gatherings that would come under the umbrella as "New Age". Whether these groups will have staying power remains to be seen.

Increased access to the internet is probably responsible for this more secular movement away from any religious spirituality whatsoever. All the major religions have extensive websites but clearly these sites are unable to persuade Mexico's skeptical youth. Perhaps it is a trend that cannot be reversed.

As a retired tourist you should feel free to express your spirituality without any sort of religious repercussion. Most Mexicans are very tolerant when it comes to religion and feel that it is a personal decision.

However, it might be best for you to keep your religious opinions to yourself as you become familiar with your new country. Mexicans may be tolerant but they are also very sensitive and there are limits.

Many older Mexicans will say good-bye by saying "Vaya con Dios"...go with God. Whether you go with God or not, it is in your best interest to be respectful, low key and respect everyone else's God.

82. Regions and Regional Variation

If you travel to different areas in Mexico you will notice how regions are distinct. Sometimes just going for a short drive will take you to an entirely different region with a different culture.

If you travel between major cities you will often notice how little traffic there is; most traffic is commercial tractor trailers. That is because Mexicans tend to stay closer to home, travel less and tend to remain in the areas where they were born. This trend is changing somewhat but it is still the norm.

Mass media, especially TV, have exposed a national culture to even those that live in remote areas. This homogenization process is not as extensive as in the U.S., but it is a trend. Many Mexicans lament the loss of their regional identities but there is not much that can be done about it. The lure of the modern world and technology is especially appealing to young people.

Still, you will notice that many areas maintain their identities and for the traveler this provides endless adventure and exploration opportunities.

In the north, the border cities and northern states tend to be more like Texas, Arizona, New Mexico and California. The close proximity and mixing of cultures make the Sinaloans dress like Texans and vice versa.

Further into the interior the regions become more isolated with indigenous cultures being very noticeable. The Tarahumara in Chihuahua, the Yaqui in Sonora and the Huastesco in Hidalgo, Tamaulipas and Veracruz come to mind.

The further south one goes the more isolated are the regions, especially in the mountainous areas. Oaxaca has a mix of indigenous peoples. In Chiapas and the Yucatan, the Maya predominate.

With the change in regions comes a change in cuisine. The Huasteca region is famous for its green and red salsas on enchiladas but the Maya do not eat salsas per se, only a type of salsa made from the habanero pepper.

Native indigenous languages such as Nahuatl, Huasteco and Maya are still spoken but are disappearing. Spanish is spoken in all public schools so most Mexican children now prefer to speak Spanish.

Dress and native clothing also varies from region to region but now it is rare to see younger indigenous folk not wearing ball caps, t-shirts and jeans.

As a retiree or tourist you will sometimes find these differences overwhelming but at the same time a constant source of interest and fascination. As you absorb little bits of these cultures you will find yourself not only having fun but at least on some level living a richer and fuller life.

If variety is the spice of life, then viva la diferencia!

83. Seasons, Weather and Climate

Mexico has four seasons though in some regions the seasons are indistinguishable.

In the south, snow and ice only occur on the highest mountain peaks. In the winter time, snow and ice storms can hit the northern states but usually the accumulation amounts are small. Snow is more frequent in the northern Sierra Madre mountain ranges especially in the western Sierra Madres.

During winter, strong cold fronts can sweep down from Canada and the U.S. and reach as far as the Yucatan Peninsula and Chiapas. By U.S. and Canadian standards these storms do not pack much of punch but in Mexico where most of the year is hot or warm, the effects are hard felt.

As these cold fronts enter and the temperatures drop, clinics and hospitals are filled with patients complaining of sore throats, flu and bronchitis. Local governments distribute blankets but there is not much anyone can do.

Temperatures do tend to rise in the summer months going over 100 degrees Fahrenheit during the day in many areas. It can also be hot at night as well. In coastal areas high temperatures are often accompanied by high humidity and the effect can be stifling.

But even in summer months many mountainous areas are pleasant with warm days and cool nights. For those that simply cannot stand the summer heat and humidity, the mountainous areas offer a pleasant alternative.

Spring and fall in many areas are barely noticeable.

Rainfall tends to be higher in the summer and winter months; the winter rains often the results of cold fronts. Summer storms are not unusual in coastal areas and late afternoon thunder bursts are common in desert areas.

Hurricane season is late spring through fall. It is not unusual for hurricanes to hit in late October. The Pacific Coast does have hurricanes but they tend be in the lower intensity categories. The Gulf Coast and Yucatan are much more prone to strong hurricanes during the season.

Storms spawn off the coast of Western Africa and gain strength as they enter the warm waters of the Caribbean. If they continue to build in strength they will take two general tracks; north to Cuba, the Gulf of Mexico and Florida and the U.S. Gulf Coast or west toward the Yucatan peninsula.

The hurricanes that hit the Yucatan can be devastating. With no land barriers from Africa, these southern Caribbean hurricanes can be both large and powerful. As they slam into Mexico, Belize or Honduras the winds and floods can cause extensive damage. In recent years a number of these hurricanes have crossed the Yucatan peninsula losing strength only to re-form in the warm waters of the Gulf of Mexico.

Most strong hurricanes in the Gulf take a northerly route and hit landfall north of Vera Cruz City. The problem in this region is not so much the wind damage but the heavy rainfall hitting the eastern Sierra Madre mountain range and dumping vast amounts of water that quickly drains toward the coast. The low lying lower Gulf Coast region of Veracruz and Tabasco can suffer from severe flooding which may last for weeks. If you travel in this area after a major hurricane you will find many road closures and washed out bridges.

But heavy rainfall need not come from just hurricanes or large tropical storms; late June, July and August can have a mini-monsoon season where it rains heavily for days on end.

In Mexico City, late summer heavy rains can cause widespread flooding as drains clog and are unable to handle the flow.

In contrast, March, April and May are often drought months throughout many parts of Mexico. Wells go dry, the earth becomes cracked, cattle get thin and crops wither.

With such a vast spectrum of terrain and weather dynamics, Mexico is a land of varied climates and constantly changing weather conditions. Climatic change appears to have changed the weather in some areas but it is not known if these changes are permanent or only temporary.

In severe weather, listen to the radio and TV to find out conditions and what you should do. For normal weather ask the locals what you should expect and when.

As usual, everyone talks and complains about the weather but no one can do anything about it.

84. Sun, Sunglasses, Heat, Humidity and Staying Cool

Most of Mexico lies below the Tropic of Cancer which simply means that the sun is not only bright but because it is more directly overhead, more intense. In many areas with the weather report the weatherperson will also give a UV reading. It is not unusual for warnings to be issued with high UV concentrations. I always wear sunglasses when driving or exposed to direct sunlight. At the beach, sunglasses simply are not optional during heavy sunlight hours.

The UV problem is actually worse at higher altitudes, such as Mexico City, because the air is thinner and there is less ozone protection in the atmosphere.

Get a pair of good sunglasses with 100% UV protection.

If you are fair skinned like I am, cover up. Don't forget to cover that bald head as well and you will want to bring a good sun block lotion. When the sun is high in the sky or directly overhead or if you are in a high altitude, you can burn and blister in as little as 15 minutes of direct sunlight exposure. Never forget you are near or below the Tropic of Cancer.

With so much sun, temperatures can get toasty. In northwestern Mexico in the states of Sonora and Sinaloa, the temperatures can exceed 120 degrees Fahrenheit. Often times the area around Hermosillo will record the hottest temperatures in North America.

Some will say it's a "dry heat." It doesn't matter. When the asphalt streets start to melt, that's hot.

Elsewhere it may not be quite as hot but temperatures can get well over 100 degrees Fahrenheit. And when the humidity soars as well, sometimes approaching 100%, going outside can feel like entering a sauna.

Most Mexicans, unlike mad dogs and Englishmen, try to avoid going outside into the direct sun at peak sunlight hours. Many businesses close from 1-3 or 2-4 which is the hottest part of the day; if there are no customers on the streets, why stay open?

In urban areas or even smaller towns you can always duck into the local church or air conditioned supermarket for a brief respite. In rural areas you might want to find a good shade tree next to some water, if available.

Be very careful when walking in the brush or jungle when both the temperature and humidity are very high. Of course you will be carrying lots of water and even extra water but you may feel your skin start to get hot and your mouth feeling like it is full of cotton. This is most likely the first indication you are heading toward heat stroke.

The body can normally sweat enough water out to keep you cool but under extreme heat and humidity even sweat is not enough. The body will continue heating up until you get to the point of feeling dizzy and eventually you can pass out. If you pass out, hopefully you will fall in a shady area.

What happens is your internal organs begin to heat up and literally they start to cook. Heat stroke is serious business.

Before you pass out, find some shade, drink some water and rest. If you keep walking, your body will not have a chance to cool down. Stop for at least a half hour and then you will probably be OK for a while. If the warm skin and cotton mouth return, repeat the process.

Don't pay attention if your guide is a Maya or other indigenous person and they tell you it's OK to continue. You will be drenched in sweat and they will be hardly sweating at all.

One little trick is to do like athletes and drink lots and lots of water to hydrate before you go out. This may help to buy yourself a little more walking time.

If you come return from a lengthy stay in the heat and are exhausted, avoid drinking glass after glass of ice water. Drink room temperature water and lots of it, for at least an hour. Also avoid going into air conditioned rooms especially with very cold air; it's almost as if you will be sending your lungs and body into shock.

I personally don't care for air conditioning. Besides, continually going in and out of the cold air can cause respiratory problems. In very humid, tropical climates air conditioning units and ducts have a tendency to get moldy and need to be cleaned periodically, which they often are not. What are the health consequences of breathing air conditioned air loaded with mold spores?

I prefer to use a fan and sometimes when sleeping, two fans at cross angles blowing from the foot of the bed. If you are making a list of what to bring on your trip, be sure to add a small portable fan that you can pack away in your luggage. Fans also are good for helping blow away those pesky mosquitoes.

The real advantage you have as a retiree or tourist is you don't have to work out in the sun or in the extreme heat. Plan when you go out, drink lots of fluids and use your fan.

And of course you will want to take that afternoon siesta as well… you earned it!

85. Environment and Ecology

When Mexico was first conquered by the Spaniards, it was a country covered with deep forests, jungles and pristine deserts. Today the habitat has changed dramatically as it has in many third world countries, such as Brazil and India.

For example, in the state of Veracruz there is on only 2-3% of the original forest left; the rest has been cut down and converted into pasture land for cattle, fields for farming, and roads and streets for the hundreds of towns and cities that cover the countryside.

One only has to look at the barren land surrounding the "Pico de Orizaba", Mexico's highest point, to see how the forests have all been cut. Illegal logging, wildfires and indigent locals cutting firewood have been responsible for the devastation.

There is a small ray of hope in Mexico's youth who view the destruction as an imminent Armageddon if the situation is not reversed. And indeed, if it were not for the youth there would be no hope.

Consider the following.

Mexico City is one of the world's largest cities with an estimated population of 25 million. The metro area extends from Pachuca in the north to Toluca in the west to almost Puebla in the south. The urban axis is over one hundred miles in any direction.

The smog is so bad that on certain days the government advises its citizens to not exercise outdoors. One of the comments I have heard from my good friends the "Chilangos" is "we grew up in this air so we are accustomed to it" The pollution blows all the way to the Gulf Coast and it is an unusual day when the Volcano Popocatepetl can be seen in the south from Mexico City.

Perhaps Mexico City is beyond the point of no return, at least from the standpoint of a turnaround within several generations.

The Caribbean Coast or Riviera Maya is another example. In 1960 the population of the state of Quintana Roo was 60,000 people. Today Cancun has 1,000,000, Playa del Carmen 500,000 and Tulum 50,000.

There are 150 hotel complexes between Tulum and Cancun. As a consequence, the coral reefs off Cancun and Playa del Carmen are dead and those off Tulum are dying. The beaches of Cancun and Playa steadily erode away as the Cancun airport handles over 300 flights daily.

It's as if the very nature that brings the tourists is being killed by the tourists.

The tragedy goes on and on. One has to go the more remote jungles and mountain areas to find pristine environment. One has to wonder how much longer it will last and whether there is enough time to turn things around.

Perhaps. Mexico's youth are raising their collective voices in unison in protest against turning their country into a wasteland. Unfortunately with each passing day the odds of that happening are increasing.

As a retiree tourist guest you can do your part by practicing sound eco habits and setting the example. You will find many Mexicans will be interested in your views and experiences with recycling, water conservation and how to reduce air pollution.

It takes little to do your part and set an example. It's the least you can do for your newly adopted country.

86. Entertainment or What to Do

So you worked hard all your life so you could retire and have free time to do the things you want to do. Now it's time to implement your action plan.

It appears that entertainment comes in three varieties; that which you create for yourself, that which others create for you and that which just happens spontaneously and is not planned. This may be a simplistic way of looking at it, but in general that looks to be the way it really is.

No one knows your interests better than you do, so your first task to find the ways you entertain yourself. Examples might be reading, painting, sewing, Sudoku, crossword puzzles, cooking and so on.

For instance, if watercolors are something you really enjoy doing, you should consider getting a good set of brushes and paints before you go down. I don't paint but the wife does and over the years I have found paints, brushes and other supplies at thrift stores, estate sales, flea markets, garage sales. Etc. She loves me for it and now has a real artist studio.

I on the other hand enjoy reading at night or on a rainy day so I will always bring down several dozen books from the U.S.

Figure out what you are interested in and plan accordingly. That way you will always have something to do.

Depending on where you live, you will also have many local events available to you.

When we stay in the country, we go for hikes, visit neighbors, look at flowers and insects, shoot videos, do arts and crafts, fish and so on. Sometimes we just go exploring in the jungle just to see what we can find. We are never disappointed.

When we are in the city, we like to visit the museums, art galleries, attend cultural events, etc. The larger the city the more activities you will find. In fact, a city like Vera Cruz or Cancun will have something you can go and do every day of the year.

For us planning one event a day is enough. That way we can sleep in, go somewhere new or just see what happens. Some of the best times you will have are those times where you did not have something planned but just let the spontaneous happen.

As you add to your repertoire of things to do you can go back and do the things that you enjoy the most. For instance, you may find a favorite art gallery and go back on a monthly basis to see the new exhibits.

As you explore you can develop new interests. This is not only fun but also helps keep the brain active and going strong. Many Mexican towns have squares or "zocalos" where people congregate, families visit, kids play, musicians play for tips and vendors hawk their wares. Cities like Papantla or Valladolid have great zocalos and are a source of entertainment in themselves.

If you have a favorite restaurant or coffee shop you can stop by on the way and make it a real outing.

These types of entertainment are not only cheap or free but you may find them more entertaining than spending more money on something that is not as much fun.

So why not develop a new interest? You might find you really like it and get some positive brain plasticity as a bonus.

The point is to be active and not sit around waiting for something to happen. Get out and about. Meet new people and develop new interests.

You worked hard all your life to get to this point. May as well take advantage of it, no?

87. Sports

Mexico is the land of soccer. Period. Mexicans tend to be as fanatical as any sports fans anywhere and most of that fanaticism is directed toward soccer or "futbol."

Even before they can walk, little boys play kicking the ball with their fathers and older brothers. At some point it is every boy's dream to become a soccer star and play for the national team or one of the popular professional soccer teams: Cruz Azul, America, Chivas de Guadalajara or Rayados de Monterey.

Local soccer leagues are formed in essentially every locale from infancy through middle age. Those very best players "graduate" from these local leagues and sign a contract with a professional league farm team. Most towns of any size will have their own team and the bigger cities have professional teams that belong to the various levels of professional competition.

The top professional or first division teams have a regular season which terminates in a playoff which determines the national champion. Radio, TV and newspapers devote much time and space to discussing these teams, their players and coaches and a seemingly endless series of faults and merits.

And of course every four years the national team competes in the North American World Cup Elimination to qualify for the World Cup or worldwide soccer tournament. It seems that when the team is successful exuberance abounds but when the team fails then there is much anguish, soul searching and criticism of the national character.

Baseball is also popular but runs a far distant second to soccer in popularity. Soccer players tend to be lean and adept and baseball players muscle bound and overweight. The national professional league has its playoffs and "World Series" each summer.

Boxing, basketball, American football, tennis as well as track and field are also popular but much less so.

Most fans tend to follow soccer and several other sports and many fans are quite knowledgeable about American sports. American football, baseball, and basketball can be seen on cable and certain broadcast stations and it seems that these sports are slowly gaining in popularity, especially from immigrants that have returned back home from Mexico.

But no sport rivals soccer and it will probably stay that way indefinitely.

I watch the national team play international games especially those that involve the World Cup. I will usually watch some of the games in the final nationwide soccer tournament but seldom watch games in the regular season.

I do like to watch the NFL playoffs, Superbowl, NBA Finals and World Series which are readily available in Mexico, especially on cable TV. In recent years some of the more hyped boxing matches have been broadcast nationally and are free.

If you are a sports fan and want to see the game on computer, beware. Many of the playoff and championship games that are streamed for free on the internet are not available in Mexico. Even if you access a website with free streaming in the U.S., you will not be able to view it in Mexico, at least unless you pay a fee.

I am often asked who I pull for in the international soccer matches. My answer is somewhat simplistic and perhaps a bit evasive. When Mexico plays, I pull for Mexico. When the U.S. plays, I pull for the U.S. When Mexico plays against the U.S., I pull for the winner.

Ah, the sporting life…

88. Hunting and Fishing

Many, many years ago I did some small bird hunting in the Eastern Sierra region of Mexico but have not hunted since. Hunting is pretty well limited to the very northern sections of Mexico and only for deer and some birds such as ducks and white wing doves. For my taste, it's not worth the hassle. If you are a hunter you are just as well off going to areas in Texas or New Mexico.

Hunting is expensive and includes a long list of requirements. Those that do hunt usually find brokers to do the paperwork. Costs can exceed $1000 U.S.; the permit itself runs about $500 U.S.

You are limited to what you can shoot, where you can shoot, and what kinds of guns and ammo you can bring in. I have spoken with duck hunters who rave about the doves in Tamaulipas but if it's not your idea of fun then best pass it by. If you do decide to hunt, do all your research, find the proper contacts and follow the limits and requirements to the letter.

You will notice that hunting is not permitted down in the interior where bigger game do exist. These game, such as the jaguar, are strictly off limits.

Bringing in unregistered guns and ammunition means prison. For my peso, don't do it.

Fishing is much more open but there are still many restrictions. Fresh water fishing is on the wane as rivers and lakes become polluted, dammed and over fished. Virtually all fresh water fish consumed is now farmed.

Ocean fishing is still good but is also facing problems with pollution and over fishing. The Gulf of Mexico has been especially hard hit in recent years as fish populations have dropped.

It may seem paradoxical that so many fishing restrictions apply to tourists while Mexican commercial fishing continues to overfish.

Resorts such as Cozumel and Cabo San Lucas are known for their sport fishing charters and although it has been many years since I have gone, the reports are still that the fishing is very good. Charters in these resorts are comparable in price to charters in Florida and California so make sure you bring your credit card.

Like scuba diving, the hunters and fisher folk bring in big bucks or pesos and so these sports are heavily promoted by the offices of tourism. A backpacker in the jungle might spend twenty or thirty dollars in a day but a scuba diver, hunter or charter fisherman can spend hundreds of dollars a day.

Obviously the offices of tourism both local, state and federal are like tourism promoters everywhere in that they follow the money trail.

As you can see I don't hunt anymore and seldom fish either. We both prefer the jungles, forests, deserts, museums, and ruins in natural settings. Along with whatever animals happen to be around.

However if you do decide to hunt or fish you should be aware of the regulations and requirements.

89. Ruins and Museums

Ruins are almost everywhere in Mexico. In certain regions such as the Gulf Coast or the Yucatan, ruins are literally everywhere.

All ruins are not alike. Some are more developed than others. Many ruins such as Coba and Edzna have only been partially excavated, perhaps only the central portion or "acropolis" of the ancient city.

Most ruins charge admission but not all ruins have equal admission prices. Chichen Itza, Teotihuacan, Tajin and Tulum can cost up to $20 U.S. or more per entry. Smaller ruins such as Chachoben, La Venta or Ek Balaam will cost $5 U.S. or less per entry. You will notice that you as a tourist may be charged much more per ticket than a Mexican. But you will also notice that local indigenous folk are often not charged at all.

For my taste, the tourist sites such as Chichen or Teotihuacan are over promoted and over visited. Bus load after bus load of tourists stream into these sites. I once calculated that a new busload of sightseers entered Chichen every 30 seconds during the peak afternoon hours. That's a lot of turistas!

That is not to say you shouldn't go to these sites -- you should. But just be aware that as the day wears on the tourist traffic picks up and you may have to wait in long lines to see certain attractions, just like Disneyland.

So it's better to go early to avoid the hordes. It is also better to go early to avoid the heat. Even in the cooler winter months it can get very toasty at a ruin like Chichen.

Wear a hat, bring extra water, pack a lunch and take numerous rest stops along the way. If you visit a major ruin, plan on a full day.

Museums are located in many major and smaller cities now. They are primarily art, indigenous and historical. Check the local tourist promotion listings to see what is in your area and the hours of operation. If you have guests and live in the city, be sure to take them to see a museum or two.

Don't forget to take bottled water and pack a lunch. Many larger museums have cafeteria areas that sell food and drinks where you can also sit down for a good rest and eat your sack lunch. Just like the ruins, there is a limit to how long and far you can walk without completely wearing out, so pace yourself.

For the best days and times to visit both ruins and museums, ask the locals. Many ruins and museums will have “free days” when they charge no entrance fee. Of course there may be more visitors but if you can save a $20 entry fee, why not? And with free admission, you can also go back numerous times. Besides, many of the ruins and museums just have too much to see in one visit.

If you have internet access you can search the ruin or museum for fees, hours and days of operation. You can also search for information on specific sights and exhibits. If you return for multiple visits you can learn something new each time you go.

When we go to ruin or museum we like to go early, stay as late as we can and not plan anything else for the day. That way you can go day after day if you like and not get too worn out.

Ruins and museums are open to expose you to the past in ways which you could not otherwise experience. It is up to you to take full advantage!

90. Art, Cultural Events and "la Casa de Cultura"

One real advantage of retiring and having free time is that you can take advantage of art and cultural events that you could not do when working. Mexico offers a vast array of art and activities to choose from.

In recent years almost all small cities and large towns have established a "Casa de Cultura" or House of Culture. These Casas de Cultura have a physical location usually in the center of town or other prominently accessible area.

They will have a permanent art collection and rotating temporary exhibits emphasizing local artists and artisans. The larger ones will have theatre and skits done by local actors and schoolchildren. You should check their schedule for dates and times.

Some of the larger Casas de Culturas also will have bookstores which can carry an interesting assortment of art and cultural books. Of course these books will be in Spanish but since you are learning Spanish you can do two things at once.

Like many aspects of Mexico, art can be divided into Pre-Colombian, Classical and Contemporary art. The Maya hieroglyphs or Huastec statues would be considered Pre-Colombian and art works by Diego Rivera, Frida Kahlo and Rufino Tamayo would come under the category of contemporary art.

Many cities and larger towns sponsor numerous cultural events often tied to local celebrations and holidays such as Mexican Independence Day and Christmas. These events are fun and although perhaps not of Broadway caliber they are free and provide a nice outing.

Over the years I have become interested in Pre-Colombian art and the connection with classical and contemporary art. I'm certainly not an expert by any means but it is interesting for instance to see the connection between the Maya jaguar statuary of Quintana Roo and modern artists' interpretation and integration of the jaguar gods in contemporary works.

One of the ways I keep improving my "hobby" is to search for relevant art books on both sides of the border. I have found some excellent illustrated books on Pre-Columbian art in flea markets and antique stores in Texas and California. Some of these books would cost $50-60 in bookstores but can be had for $2-5 secondhand. On rainy days we enjoy just taking out the books and thumbing through them.

If you continue to read and study and develop an interest in Mexican art and culture you will be surprised to find out how much you effortlessly learn over time. It will also give you talking points when you strike up a conversation at a fiesta or meal with a Mexican that is interested in art. You will find these connoisseurs not only surprised at your interest and knowledge but also willing to share what they know with you, such as recommending books and exhibits you can review.

The interesting thing about art and culture is you can enter at any level. It does not matter if you are a novice or "professional", art is for everyone. The very wealthy may collect art as a hobby and the pretentious may collect art to show off, but you can "own" any piece of art by simply appreciating it at your very own level.

You will also find that some cities such as Playa del Carmen, Mexico City and Jalapa are meccas for artists. Artists from all over the country congregate there to create and sell their works. Galleries do not charge admission so you can feel free to walk in and browse. Some areas have regular days when artists display and sell their works.

Art and culture is not only fun but enlightening as well. It makes our lives a little richer each time we are exposed to it. Make it a point to at least once a week engage in some cultural activity. It costs little or nothing and you will find the experience both rewarding and fun.

91. Holidays, Fiestas and Celebrations

Mexicans love a good party. It really doesn't matter for what; any reason for getting together is good enough to celebrate.

Christmas Eve, Christmas Day, New Year's Eve and Day of the Kings or January 6 are the big holidays at the ending and beginning of the year. This season is started by La Guadalupana or Virgin Mary tribute on December 12.

After December 12 "las Posadas" or individual parties start and run up to Christmas Eve. These parties pay tribute to the Mary and Joseph, Jesus' parents, as they searched for a place to rest or "posada" ending in the now famous manger scene or Natividad. This is the most festive time of the year.

Perhaps the biggest holiday fiesta is Christmas Eve or "Noche Buena". Traditionally this is when Mexicans celebrate Christmas with their families including the biggest meal of the year at night, often around midnight.

In the old days Christmas was a simple affair with little or no gift giving. Gifts were given to children on January 6 or "Santos Reyes" who would leave their shoes out the night before in hopes of getting some gifts. This tradition is slowly being taken over by Santa Claus, the Christmas tree and gift giving on Christmas Day.

Many Mexicans lament the loss of the older traditions but it's hard to fight Santa Claus and the Christmas tree.

Perhaps the most interesting holiday is November 1 or All Saints Day "Todos Santos". This is a day when families traditionally make tamales, bread and hot chocolate and go to the cemetery to honor their deceased. They will meticulously clean the gravesites and place elaborate wreaths on the tombstones.

In their homes they will build altars with marigolds and memorabilia of the deceased. Children will return home to their place of birth and friends stop by for a chat and a tamale.

This tradition is now being overtaken by Halloween, costumes and trick or treating. Children find it impossible to resist dressing up and getting a sack full of candy.

Other holidays of lesser importance such as Valentine's Day are celebrated but with much less fanfare.

Political or national holidays are also celebrated but tend to be more community oriented with parades and local dances. In recent years Mardi Gras has become popular as towns and cities stagger their celebration dates so they can attend the celebrations in nearby towns.

Religious celebrations include First Communions, Baptisms and Marriages. These celebrations will include a sit down meal. Marriage receptions can be somewhat more elaborate with a band and special attention paid to the bride and groom.

One of the biggest and most formal fiestas is the "quincenera" or a young girl's fifteenth birthday. This is a "coming out" party announcing the girl's transition from girlhood to womanhood. These fiestas can be very elaborate with formal dresses, dances, flower arrangements, etc. Fathers can spend a lot of money on these fiestas.

Birthdays are also celebrated usually with cake and a piñata. The men drink beer and the women gossip and all have a good time. If you have a large, extended family there can be a steady stream of birthday parties.

In fact there can be a steady stream of fiestas throughout the year. If you are invited to a fiesta you should definitely go! Some of the best times you will have will be at these parties; even the relatively poor manage to have a good time when they have a fiesta. It is a good way to meet new people, practice Spanish, learn new customs and traditions, dance, try new foods and just have a good time.

Depending on the event, you can take a small gift, something to eat or something to drink.

Most fiestas are not extravagant affairs so don't feel obligated to buy an expensive gift or take lots of food or drink. Dress up in your better clothes, shine those dusty shoes and go and have a good time!

92. Television, Radio and Internet Streaming

One of the advantages of living in an urban area is media access.

For instance, when I am in Playa del Carmen, I can get cable TV, free antenna TV, radio and broadband internet with streaming. When I'm in the jungle at Coba, I get one TV station, no internet, some radio and not even cell phone connection unless I drive some 12 kilometers away. Where you live makes a difference.

One of the first things you should find out about an area is what sorts of media connections are available. Cable TV can sometimes be pricey because it comes bundled with a land line phone or satellite dish. Do some homework before you buy. A basic "Sky" satellite dish monthly fee will run around $15 a month and can be set up almost anywhere.

Mexican TV is probably even of lower quality than American TV, if that is possible…

There are just a few major networks owned by powerful magnates and they control the airwaves, both wave and content. Subsequently, the programming is pretty sad.

Mexicans are mesmerized by their soap operas or "telenovelas". They start around 11:00 AM and run until midnight or so. That's a lot of soaper hours. And if you don't get enough or miss a show, you can watch shows that talk about the soap operas. Soap operas even have a bigger audience than the soccer games.

The plots are basically the same for each one and after a while they start repeating themselves but what the heck. My favorite characters are the evil old ladies but then again that's me; usually I don't watch them because I make comments that aren't appreciated by serious viewers.

Even macho men watch the "telenovela" soap operas. They won't admit it, but they do.

Reality or rather fake reality shows are also popular. The fact they are so obviously fake doesn't matter; reality after all, is simply a matter of perception.

One exception are some of the news broadcasts which have interesting feature stories and good news coverage. Also in many areas now you can get a type of regional PBS educational channel that does have some good shows.

If you are serious about learning Spanish, TV is a good way to tune your ear.

Most of the radio is not that great either though there are some interesting programs on the public radio station. You may also find it interesting that there are some American oldies channels that play some rather esoteric oldies, something you might not expect.

The problem with most commercial radio and TV is that it is simply filled with ads. And they keep repeating the same ads over and over. Sometimes there are so many commercial ads you lose track of the show.

Another comment on TV. You may find it strange that many Mexicans turn on their televisions when they get up in the morning, leave them on all day and fall asleep with them at night. After a while the noise gets really irritating.

Especially during meal times. Don't be surprised if you are invited over to dinner and your guests have the TV blaring the entire meal. Go figure.

Restaurants are the same way. Customers will eat their food with eyes fixated on a loud TV show; it doesn't matter what show, any show will do. That's reality for you...

You can also get TV programming via internet streaming, the clear advantage being you can pick what you want to watch. You have to have a really good internet connection which is not that common in Mexico. If the signal is not strong, the picture and audio stops and starts intermittently and you have to fill in the blanks yourself. Of course if you have a creative type of personality...

We seldom watch TV and listen to the radio only for short periods of time. You be the judge. Especially if you are learning Spanish, radio and TV can be a great way to get your ear tuned in.

Then again, forget everything I said if you love soap operas. You will be in media heaven...

93. Movies, Theaters and YouTube

Movie theaters are located in most cities throughout Mexico. In major shopping centers you can find current American movies; sometimes dubbed in Spanish or subtitled in English. Even in these modern theaters you will probably pay less than half what you would pay in a comparable theater in the U.S. Early afternoon matinees are a bit cheaper.

You can also rent movies at video rental stores but most Mexicans don't bother. Pirated movie DVDs can be had for 10 pesos (80 cents U.S.) so why rent. Passing them around among friends makes the cost even cheaper.

An even better bargain if you have a decent internet connection is YouTube. Almost all older Mexican movies are now available for free on YouTube. If you have a favorite actor such as Cantinflas or Pedro Infante, simply type them in on Search and you will get a listing of available films. A simple cable hook up to your big screen and away you go. If the weather is stormy you can watch movie after movie right in your apartment or house.

Every time I watch an Elsa Aguirre movie I get weak knees.

The Golden Era of Mexican movies was from the late 1930's through the late 1950's. Literally thousands of good movies were made; movies with good plots and great scenery. These films were shot all over Mexico on location so you get a tour as well as a glimpse back into the past.

Interestingly there were hundreds of movies made based on history so the student of Mexico can not only be entertained by a good story but learn some history as well.

You will notice that some of the idioms used in the older movies are out of date but by and large the scripts would be almost identical if used today. If you want to improve your Spanish, watching these older movies is a great way to do it.

By the late 1970's the industry was on the skids and for the next 30 or so years there was a "dead period"; at times with as little as four new movies coming out of Mexico per year. Quality dropped and so did movie attendance. Most of the films made were violent, schlocky, and low quality. In the past ten years there has been a resurgence of sorts with less violence and better quality.

One interesting way to watch a movie in English is to read the subtitles in Spanish as the English is spoken. Another interesting way is to watch your favorite American actors dubbed in Spanish.

More recent movies seem to fall into two categories: seriously serious and goofy funny. I actually like the silly ones because the humor is sometimes so ridiculous it actually is funny and so much slang is thrown in that you can begin to pick it up. Sort of reminds me of the Three Stooges or Laurel and Hardy.

The serious movies can be tearjerkers and a bit depressing and I have to admit that I generally don't watch them. As the Mexicans say, better to laugh than cry.

In that genre I also am embarrassed to admit that I also like to watch "Picardia" or off color films. They really aren't X-rated and often only get a weak r-rating but they are so ridiculous they seem funny. At least to me and many Mexicans as well as they are some of the most popular movies made.

OK, OK so it's not all highbrow and literary and redeeming, inspirational, uplifting and all that stuff. But movies are for fun and entertainment and not just for spiritual enlightenment, right?

Admittedly my tastes leave something to be desired but you are going to like what you like anyway, regardless of what I say. But by "losing" ourselves in a good movie for a couple of hours we humans feel transposed into worlds we can only imagine. That's why movies are such fun.

And hey, after all, it's only a movie…

94. Cantinas, Casinos, Discos, Nightclubs and Men's Clubs

Many years ago I frequented the cantinas but in recent years I no longer go. Perhaps it's a factor of age. Or perhaps it's that I no longer drink as much beer as I used to.

Cantinas throughout Mexico are almost exclusively for men. It is a place where they go to see their friends, sometimes get drunk and talk freely about their wives, children, girlfriends, lovers and whatever else they care to say. There is an unwritten code of ethics that says what goes on in cantina stays in the cantina.

If you are female you should know that the only types of women that go into these cantinas are barmaids and prostitutes or both. This is not making a moral judgment but simply a statement of fact. Rightly or wrongly, if you are female and enter one of these cantinas you will be viewed as a barmaid or more likely a prostitute. Enter at your own risk.

In recent years Casinos have proliferated to the point where most major cities and many smaller cities have them. These casinos are filled with slot machines and other coin machines which have grown in popularity in recent years. You will also find betting on horse races and sporting events with large screens showing the odds and events, Las Vegas style. There are some card tables visible but most of the heavy betting takes place in back rooms.

Drinks are expensive and one has to go through security before entering. If you are on a fixed income, casinos are not your cup of tea.

Discos are found in resort areas like Cancun and Puerto Vallarta. The music is loud, the drinks expensive and if you are over 30 you will find yourself in a minority. Like nightclubs, heavy drinking is the norm and if you are a female you should be careful.

Nightclubs usually get going after midnight and will operate into the morning hours. They tend to be very expensive and often filled with "seedy" characters that will look at you strangely. Again, be wary.

Men's Clubs or Strip Clubs have also grown in recent years. They are usually located on the outskirts of town and have high walls with heavy security. I don't go into them so cannot recommend what you should or should not do. The big attraction is the "laptop" dancing which is very popular among middle aged males. Such is life.

In many areas that are violence prone, particularly in the northern States, night life can be quite risky. As usual you should ask before you go; if the locals don't dare go then you should stay away too.

For many people going out late at night into the clubs and bars is a prime source of entertainment. You should be aware that it will always be expensive and there are certain risks involved. Use your common sense and good judgment.

95. Police, Soldiers, Checkpoints, Traffic Cops and the Law

The three levels of government -- municipal, state and federal -- each have their own police force. You will hear many "stories" about the Mexican police, some true and some not true. In the past decade there has been a concerted effort to eradicate corruption with police but most Mexicans will still tell you there is much work to be done.

The good news for the retired tourist is that police tend to leave the tourist alone. If a complaint is lodged against a police officer by a tourist, the officer could lose his job. In all the many years I have traveled in Mexico I have never really been harassed by the police. I have been stopped and questioned in the past and even asked for money, but nothing serious.

The best way to avoid problems with the police is not break any laws or do anything wrong.

You will see soldiers in dark green uniforms patrolling highways and even local streets. Sometimes they will wear masks and they will be armed. I have never been entirely certain why they will appear as if they are ready to shoot but it probably has something to do with demonstrating force.

The marines or "Marina" are Mexico's elite force and wear grey uniforms.

If you travel you will encounter checkpoints by police, soldiers and less frequently by state police. Sometimes they will ask to see your papers but usually not. If you drive, they may ask you to open your trunk. They may ask you simple questions such as where are you from, where are you going, what is your work, etc. These questions are simply to determine if you are a "legitimate" tourist or not. Like customs officials they are trained to look for nervousness or other indications you are up to something.

Of course you are simply a tourist and will be motioned to pass through.

Traffic cops are another matter. If you drive and have non-Mexican plates, you can expect to be stopped. They will ask to see your vehicle and tourist papers, may inspect the vehicle permit sticker on your windshield and may ask to see your license. You are required to show your license but are not required to hand it over to them. By regulation they are checking your license to see if it is valid.

Unfortunately they may at times assert you committed an infraction even though you did not. They may also ask you for money. Stay calm. Keep repeating that you are a tourist and broke no laws. Sometimes they will keep asking for money but lower the amounts. Keep insisting politely you are a tourist and broke no laws. Eventually they tell you to move on.

These traffic cops can be a pain but are a reality when driving in Mexico. Fortunately there are efforts by municipalities and states to clean up these forces. But you eventually will be stopped so expect it and remain calm and respectful.

The best course of action as a retired tourist is to never break any laws. Period. The old saying that you are guilty in Mexico until proven innocent is no longer completely true. This old precept has now been replaced by the law of "common sense." Most police and traffic cops will sometimes admonish a tourist but usually let them go. Being a tourist has its advantages; Mexicans sometimes are not so lucky.

For instance, if you as a tourist are drunk and unruly on the Quinta Avenida in Playa del Carmen, you will be escorted to your hotel room and told to stay there. If a Mexican citizen is drunk and unruly in the same place, they will be escorted to jail.

Of the millions of tourists that visit Cancun yearly, only about a dozen formal complaints are filed. This is because complaints are taken care of before they become formal. Harassing tourists is a big no-no.

Mexico essentially does everything it can to welcome you as a tourist and to make sure stay is a pleasant one. As a guest it is in your best interest to do everything you can to be courteous and stay out of trouble.

96. Corruption and the "Mordida"

When my American friends ask "why do you go to Mexico? It's so corrupt…" I have a simple reply. I say corruption is also in the USA but in different forms, such as special interest Political Action Committees (PACs) influencing legislation or "legalized corruption." Go figure. Corruption in some form is present everywhere.

True, corruption exists in Mexico and each Presidente vows to stamp it out and at times one can sense progress is being made and at other times it seems not much has changed.

As a tourist and retiree you will sometimes face corruption but unless you open a business or buy a house the corruption you face will be "lightweight," usually in the form of a "mordida" or bite.

Sometimes the police, immigration officials or more often the transit police will ask for money when you have not done anything. Such is life and such is life in Mexico. How you deal with these requests will determine how well you adapt to Mexican life. Mexicans just shrug their shoulders; it's actually worse for them.

Officials in general are told to lay off the tourists and complaints can cost an official his or her job. If you are asked for money by an official one good tactic is to keep stalling; especially with the notorious traffic cops. Usually if they keep insisting the amount they are asking for continues to go down, say from 1000 pesos to 600 pesos to 200 pesos. Whether or not you pay is a matter of your good judgment.

Many tourists as well as many Mexicans say flat out you should never give any official any bribe under any circumstances as that is the only way corruption can be wiped out. This is the moral high ground and admirable but on the other hand if you get an official angry they can create an even bigger hassle for you, a hassle you definitely do not need.

Most Mexicans will tell you to argue with the official and get them to accept the lowest "mordida" possible so as to avoid other problems.

As you can see, there are no easy answers.

In bigger matters, such as business contracts or a house or condominium contract, "mordidas" are accepted as a cost of doing business. If you want to get something done, you will have to pay the "mordida" to move things along. Without the “mordida” things tend to get bogged down forever in endless red tape; Twilight Zone and black hole are two analogies that come to mind.

But since you most likely will not being doing any large contracts, this should not be a problem.

On the plus side Mexico is doing many things to try and reduce and eventually eliminate corruption. When I first started going to Mexico, it was not uncommon to have to pay the immigration officials “mordidas” to get permits and go through inspections. That has changed. Now there are signs at the border saying that if you offer immigration officials bribes, you can be prosecuted. I’ve never heard of that happening, but there has been a distinct shift in policy and procedure.

Unfortunately there are no hard and fast rules for what is best to do. Some tourists are so incensed at being stopped by traffics cops and asked for money, that they refuse to come back.

Over the years I have been stopped many times and often under pretenses that were obviously contrived, such as the speed limit is 15 kilometers per hour on curves, when it is not posted. Or I was not wearing my seat belt properly. Or you need a special insurance policy to drive in our city.

Each time I have to deal with this and it will not stop me from traveling to Mexico. Hopefully it will not stop you either.

Be aware, expect to be stopped and know in advance what you are going to say as well as what not to say. It’s all a part of the adaptation process.

97. Violence and Insecurity

No discussion of current day Mexico would be complete without mentioning the problems of crime, violence and insecurity. The mass media worldwide have covered these topics and life has certainly changed in Mexico. Whether these changes are permanent or not remains to be seen.

Of course crime occurs everywhere, even in the California suburb where we lived for many years. But that is little consolation.

The figures in Mexico are staggering; tens of thousands dead, major urban areas under crime syndicate mandated curfews, entire police forces fired for complicity, etc. Those stories are true as far as they go.

It also seems the violence tends to ebb and flow and with occasional flare-ups. You can search the internet find out what is the latest status. The U.S. State Department and State of Texas issue warnings but neither are entirely reliable.

The first point to realize that the vast majority of Mexicans are good people and law abiding citizens. Period. The media often relay the message that all young people carry machine guns and drive Hummers. Just not true.

The truth is virtually all of the deaths in the cartel drug wars are between cartels as they vie for territorial control. That is the simple fact. When large numbers of bodies are found, the authorities are well aware of who has been killed and often will not even attempt to identify the bodies.

Of the many that are killed almost none are tourists. Those tourists that are killed, usually were in the wrong place at the wrong time. A very, very small number of tourists that have been killed might have been involved in some way with organized crime.

The cartels have no interest in harming tourists nor regular law abiding Mexican citizens for that matter. It serves no purpose. In the case of foreigners, extensive investigations by the Mexican Attorney General's Office are standard procedure. In the case of regular Mexican citizens, nothing is to be gained by generating ill will from the general populace.

In fact, many of the Cartel leaders are considered heroes, much the same as Robin Hood.

It is also important to distinguish between "normal" crime and drug cartel crime. Normal crime can occur essentially anywhere, though violent crimes are much more prevalent in urban areas. Small towns in rural areas have very low crime rates.

Cartel related violence is largely restricted to areas where territories are contested, or primarily in the border and northern portion of Mexico. Kidnapping, extortions and other crimes almost never involve tourists. That's not to say it does not happen, but it is not common.

Tourists are also protected in resort areas for obvious reasons; crimes against tourists are bad for the tourist industry, which as we have seen is the number one industry in Mexico.

If you are considering retiring in an area, the first place to start is ask the local populace what they think. If they tell you to stay out of certain clubs and bars, don't go. In the border areas, if a taxi driver says don't go out after 9:00 PM, don't go out.

If you plan on driving to Mexico, don't take the Mercedes. Don't wear lots of jewelry, fancy clothes, flash money, and brag or tell everybody about your fabulously wealthy uncle in Omaha. Unfortunately highway assaults are on the rise though tourists tend to not be targeted.

Mind your own business, don't get drunk in public, don't mess with someone else's spouse, avoid badmouthing anyone in public, act courteously and always wear your better behavior.

In short, use common sense and you should be fine. If you have no common sense, drink too much or simply must show off to feel your importance, you should probably go to Miami Beach, Las Vegas or Honolulu instead where you will fit right in.

98. Newspapers, Internet Newspapers and Prensaescrita.com

Newspapers are a great way to learn about local, state, regional and national events and issues. They are also an excellent way to learn Spanish.

You can buy the Sunday paper which is bigger and read it throughout the week. You may not find the society news or the soccer news interesting but take a look anyway. Don't forget to look at the ads.

When you come across words of interest or words that are used repeatedly and don't know their meanings, look them up in your pocket dictionary. A good way of getting out and about is buy the newspaper and sit down with a coffee at the local coffee shop. You will find coffee shops are a place where local business people and politicians meet, greet and do business.

When you get tired of reading the newspaper you can read the people.

Of course the internet has changed the way newspapers are read and distributed. All newspapers of any size have internet additions. My favorite website is www.prensaescrita.com which has the websites of newspapers from all over the world.

Click on Mexico and then click on the state which you want to read the newspapers. Each major city has at least several papers while Mexico City has several dozen. If you get tired of reading in Spanish you can also look at the Herald in Mexico City which is in English. But remember, by reading the Spanish language papers you are also learning Spanish at the same time.

When I have the time and a good internet connection, I read a dozen or so papers off prensaescrita.com. The great thing about prensaescrita.com is you don't have to remember the paper's website address or do a search. You can also read the newspapers of other countries throughout the world including many English language papers.

You can bookmark, save or cut and paste articles you find of interest. You can then archive these articles in categories or folders for future reference. Over time as your Spanish improves and you become more familiar with the online papers, you can scan and skim more newspapers that cover your areas of interest.

Whenever I am in Tampico I get the "El Sol de Tampico." The Sunday edition has a great comics page (of prime importance), many regional articles of interest and a number of editorialists that are first rate.

Of course each paper will have its own slant and you will be surprised how outwardly biased some are to one political party or the other. After all, newspapers are a business.

You may also be surprised to find how extensive the society and club sections are. These social events such as weddings are essentially paid advertising. If you want to show off that expensive wedding dress you bought, it will cost you a pretty peso. You might ask who cares about all those high society photos and the answer is simple; those in the photos. Newspapers, like any business, follow the money trail.

Some papers do have good coverage of local cultural events so be sure to check them out. Cities like Playa del Carmen have weekly cultural events free to the public so be sure to mark those on your busy agenda calendar.

Stay informed, learn about your area, learn Spanish and follow your interests by reading the papers regularly.

And don't forget to read the people too…

99. Mexico's Future

Mexico always appears to be at a crossroads and it is certainly at a crossroads now. One hundred years after the Mexican Revolution, Mexico has still not been able to resolve its major problems.

By official government statistics, over half the population remains in poverty. Over half of the country's wealth is concentrated in the wealthiest ten families, a wealth distribution differential that is as wide as any on Earth.

To address many of Mexico's pressing problems, Mexico's current President, Enrique Pena Nieto, has proposed a series of 11 major reforms that are designed to transform the country. The reforms have been passed by the Mexican Legislature and are now in the implementation phase.

By the President's own admission, many of these reforms will take years to realize and the outcomes are uncertain. Many Mexicans are certain this is the correct path but many others are doubtful of the results.

But the solutions appear to be only partly realizable through political reforms. Some of solutions, such as corruption and lack of productivity, require social and cultural changes that are even less certain than political changes.

Subsequently, many of the changes will come on an individual level and this will not only take time but most likely new generations to accomplish. The good news is we humans are great at adapting to crises; the bad news is we humans are change resistant when a crisis does not exist.

Like many countries in the modern or "post-modern world", Mexico's future lies with its youth. And as is the rule with youth, uncertainty is more the rule than the exception.

For the outsider, visitor and tourist, these rapid social and cultural developments can be both unnerving and fascinating. The Modern World of the 21st is a true paradox and Mexican society is no different.

No matter what direction Mexican society takes, the outsider that acculturates and thrives must adapt to society as it is. One can express one's opinions best by setting an example and avoid problems by avoiding open criticism and confrontation. Each of us has to search our own soul and determine whether we can adapt or not. If you anticipate you will not be able to adapt, perhaps it's best to stay home and deal with the familiar.

But go ahead and take a look. Be bold. Nothing is gained by being timid and staying in your cocoon. If you find out it's not for you then you understand that it's not for everybody anyway.

It's takes a certain mindset and personality to go to a new land and new culture. Your task is to take a good look at yourself and see if it is for you.

Epilogue: Putting It All Together, the Big Decision and the Next Step

Now it's time to put the pieces together. You should have enough information to come to at least a preliminary decision.

Usually we humans don't make a change unless we can see a clear advantage over the status quo or what we are currently doing. Ideally you should be able to see if retiring in Mexico is in your best interest or not. It's not rocket science.

However, you may see a number of real advantages but still have doubts. Perhaps your doubts are more emotional than rational and uncertainty looms over your consideration.

OK. You don't have to decide yea or nay; it doesn't have to be a black and white. There is another alternative.

And that is to go down for a longer period and see how it feels; look at all the aspects of your decision. Fill in the blanks and connect the dots on the information you still need to make a decision.

Or stay for six months, travel around and really get a feel for what it is like.

Then go back to your home and mull it over.

Perhaps it really isn't for you; making such a big decision is beyond your capability at the moment or maybe you just feel the timing isn't just right. Just because it works for me and 2,000,000 other Americans doesn't mean it will work for you. As the saying goes, there are no guarantees in life.

Maybe you feel that simply going down for a month or two each year during the cold winter months and laying on the beach is good enough. Many tourists feel that way.

Or maybe you decide your job isn't so bad after all and you just don't think you should make such a leap at this time. Or maybe you wouldn't know what to do with so much free time.

That's fine too. If you have real doubts then it probably wouldn't work out anyway; you would have a predisposition to it not working out even if you did go; a sort of self-fulfilling prophecy.

You can put this book and your research notes aside and pick them up sometime in the future. Things may change and you will see this alternative in a new light.

Then again, maybe your job isn't so great after all. Maybe the prospect of working until you die sounds less appealing as you get older. Maybe your boss really is a jerk. Maybe you want to have one last adventure before you sink back in the rocking chair and don't get up.

Maybe it feels right even though you have a lot of questions that still remain. If so, then plan your next step; only you know what that might be.

Whatever it may be, plan the next step and you are on your way. And then the next step and the next step.

I want to wish you the best in whatever you decide or don't decide. You have spent most of your life working and maybe raising your family. Now it's time to have some fun and put a little adventure into your life! There's plenty of time left for that rocking chair…

And maybe we'll meet on the beach in Playa del Carmen and we can have a beer and some fish tacos with chipotle sauce. Yummm….

See you then! Provecho….Hasta la vista!

Made in the USA
Las Vegas, NV
29 March 2024

87976926R00129